Beauty of Crowdfunding

Crowdfunding is emerging as a new source of financing for creativity and innovation. It promotes the launching and scaling of new projects for different types of creators by providing networked platforms and handy digital tools.

This book provides insight into crowdfunding and how crowdfunding contributes to our communities and society. The book includes an overview of existing discussions across different disciplines, that is, entrepreneurship, information systems, and marketing, and correlates the literature to the best crowdfunding practices.

The book begins with origins, basic notions, and antecedents of crowdfunding. In the main parts, it demonstrates the five distinguished facets of crowdfunding: creativity, diversity, balance, connection, and change. It also addresses the drawbacks of crowdfunding and subsequent outcomes of crowdfunding success. Finally, it provides a perspective on the future of crowdfunding.

Sunghan Ryu is Assistant Professor at USC-SJTU Institute of Cultural and Creative Industry in Shanghai Jiao Tong University. His research and teaching focus on IT innovations in cultural and creative domains from a business/management perspective. His current research projects revolve around crowdfunding and its impacts on creativity and innovation. He lives in Shanghai, China, with his wife and three daughters.

Routledge Frontiers of Business Management

Innovation and Internationalisation
Successful SMEs' Ventures into China
Stuart Orr, Jane Menzies, Connie Zheng and Sajeewa 'Pat' Maddumage

Technological Substitution in Asia
Ewa Lechman

China and Global Value Chains
Globalization and the Information and Communications Technology Sector
Yutao Sun and Seamus Grimes

Transformational Entrepreneurship
Edited by Vanessa Ratten and Paul Jones

Labor Relations and Human Resource Management in China
Connie Zheng

The Management of Consumer Co-operatives in Korea
Identity, Participation and Sustainability
Edited by Seungkwon Jang

Entrepreneurship, Innovation and Inequality
Exploring Territorial Dynamics and Development
Edited by Vanessa Ratten, Jose Álvarez-García and Maria de la Cruz del Rio-Rama

Innovation and Industrial Development in China
A Schumpeterian Perspective on China's Economic Transformation
Kaidong Feng

Beauty of Crowdfunding
Blooming Creativity and Innovation in the Digital Era
Sunghan Ryu

For more information about this series, please visit www.routledge.com/series/RFBM

Beauty of Crowdfunding
Blooming Creativity and Innovation in the Digital Era

Sunghan Ryu

LONDON AND NEW YORK

First published 2020
by Routledge
2 Park Square, Milton Park, Abingdon, Oxon OX14 4RN

and by Routledge
52 Vanderbilt Avenue, New York, NY 10017

Routledge is an imprint of the Taylor & Francis Group, an informa business

First issued in paperback 2021

© 2020 Sunghan Ryu

The right of Sunghan Ryu to be identified as author of this work has been asserted by him in accordance with sections 77 and 78 of the Copyright, Designs and Patents Act 1988.

All rights reserved. No part of this book may be reprinted or reproduced or utilised in any form or by any electronic, mechanical, or other means, now known or hereafter invented, including photocopying and recording, or in any information storage or retrieval system, without permission in writing from the publishers.

Trademark notice: Product or corporate names may be trademarks or registered trademarks, and are used only for identification and explanation without intent to infringe.

British Library Cataloguing-in-Publication Data
A catalogue record for this book is available from the British Library

Library of Congress Cataloging-in-Publication Data
Names: Ryu, Sunghan, author.
Title: Beauty of crowdfunding : blooming creativity and innovation in the digital era / Sunghan Ryu.
Description: Abingdon, Oxon ; New York, NY : Routledge, 2020. | Series: Routledge frontiers of business management | Includes bibliographical references and index.
Identifiers: LCCN 2019042361 (print) | LCCN 2019042362 (ebook) |
Subjects: LCSH: Crowd funding. | Creative ability in business. | New business enterprises—Finance.
Classification: LCC HG4751 .R97 2020 (print) | LCC HG4751 (ebook) | DDC 658.15/224—dc23
LC record available at https://lccn.loc.gov/2019042361
LC ebook record available at https://lccn.loc.gov/2019042362

ISBN: 978-0-367-19853-4 (hbk)
ISBN: 978-1-03-208191-5 (pbk)
ISBN: 978-0-429-24371-4 (ebk)

Typeset in Galliard
by Apex CoVantage, LLC

For my wife Soohee and daughters Jimin, Jiwon, and Jina

Contents

Preface ix
Acknowledgments x

Introduction 1

PART 1
About crowdfunding 11

1 Crowdfunding: an old story? 13
2 How crowdfunding works 16
3 Understanding the foundation of crowdfunding 21
4 What we know (and don't know) about crowdfunding 31

PART 2
Beauty of crowdfunding 37

5 Creativity 39
6 Diversity 49
7 Balance 64
8 Connection 77
9 Change 88

PART 3
Behind crowdfunding 103

10 Key challenges and drawbacks of crowdfunding 105

11 What comes next after crowdfunding 114

Epilogue: Divergence and convergence 121

Index 126

Preface

> Of life's two chief prizes, beauty and truth, I found the first in a loving heart and the second in a laborer's hand.
>
> – Khalil Gibran

In the summer of 2012, I was struggling to encounter my doctoral dissertation theme. To me, crowdfunding was like a revelation. I have wandered across business, culture, and technology and found myself with scant suspicion of the current financial systems. Many vital sectors of our society have been neglected and overlooked by the capital markets. We could have seen more creativity and innovation on a "better" ground.

I heard of crowdfunding from one of my friends who had just initiated a crowdfunding platform in Seoul, Korea. When I listened to the story, I fell into the world of crowdfunding. I thought it was beautiful, possessing beauty inside of it. What beauty? Isn't it a new platform business? This book is the record of the journey to finding the roots of my fascination on the beauty of crowdfunding.

Crowdfunding was in the toddler stage at that time. I asked to meet the team behind the representative crowdfunding platform in Korea. We met and agreed to kick-start a research project. I made mistakes and messed up many times during the project, but thanks to their tolerance and support, I received my doctoral degree in the summer of 2014. That was just the beginning. After that, I initiated a series of studies on crowdfunding. I was fortunate enough to publish some journal papers and book chapters on crowdfunding. In the meanwhile, crowdfunding seemed to enter into its childhood. A major portion of the population is familiar with the concept, but unfortunately, many overlook the true beauty of crowdfunding. I thought it was the right timing for writing this book.

It did take around a year to finish the project, which was much longer than expected. But, while working, I felt grateful as I could enjoy the two chief prizes of life: beauty and truth. I again realized my love of crowdfunding and felt alive while writing this book with my two hands.

I hope you will participate in my journey toward encountering the beauty (and truth) of crowdfunding!

Acknowledgments

I would like to thank my collaborators on the core studies, opening up the opportunities for this book and other research projects: Keongtae Kim, Jungpil Hahn, Jooyoung Park, Ayoung Suh, Sha Yang, Lian Jian, Daegon Cho, Heeseok Lee, Junyeong Lee, Jinyoung Min, Hernan Galperin, Byungho Park, Dinesh Puranam, Qing Wang, Nathaniel Ming Curran, Changwoo Suh, Manuel Wiesche, Kyungmin Choi, Miyeon Jung, Boram Kwon, and Minjoo Lee.

I am grateful to my colleagues at Shanghai Jiao Tong University (SJTU) and the University of Southern California (USC). In particular, I thank Weimin Zhang, dean of USC-SJTU Institute of Cultural and Creative Industry (ICCI), for supporting and encouraging my academic journey. I am also thankful to Shantanu Dutta and Ben Lee of USC for providing me with great resources from the USC side. I would like to thank Zhao (Lena) Feng, Jinzhang Jiang, and Ke Xue for their leadership to advance ICCI to the next level. I am also honored to work with the most enterprising colleagues at ICCI: Titus Levi, Cornelia Bogen, Pearl Wang, Wei Wang, Ouchul Hwang, Wen-shing HO, Zhou Bin, Phoebe Xu, Jordan Gamble, Travis Jeppesen, Sherwood Hu, Faye Wu, and Mo Liang.

I would also like to thank members of the staff team at ICCI who have supported my academic activities in many remarkable ways. Without their support, I could not conduct research and teach students in a wonderful environment. I have had wonderful years at ICCI getting to know and teach many outstanding students. I have learned a lot from the students.

I am particularly indebted to my PhD advisor, Young-Gul Kim, for guiding me during my incredible four years at KAIST College of Business. After graduation, he has still been coaching me how to perform as a competitive researcher and teacher and, most importantly, how to live as a good person. I am also thankful to the other members of my dissertation committee – Jaehyeon Ahn, Jaemin Jung, Suhwan Jeon, and Moonyoung Kang – for granting and supporting my academic journey. I thank the members and alumni of the Entertainment Industry Research Lab, Knowledge Management Research Center, and the Information and Media Research Center at KAIST.

I have benefited remarkably from the interaction and collaboration with the industry. Specially, I am indebted to Jaeseung Yum, founder of Tumblbug, for initiating and supporting the first of my crowdfunding research projects. Without the project, this book could not have come to life. I also thank Donggun Lee, CEO/founder of MyRealTrip, for introducing the world of crowdfunding to me. I am immensely glad that your second venture, after the crowdfunding business, is hitting the market.

Yong Ling Lam, Samantha Phua, and their team at Routledge have been remarkably professional and supportive during the whole process. I am thankful to them for granting a chance to me, a first-time author. I am also grateful to Mike McIlvain for his editorial support and feedback.

I thank my parents for always supporting me and for their unlimited love. I cannot pay back your devotion in my lifetime. I am also thankful to my in-laws for their welcome and encouragement. My brother, sisters-in-law, and brothers-in-law have provided me with remarkable support.

My three daughters, Jimin, Jiwon, and Jina, are my greatest source of enjoyment and inspiration. Their existence in my life strongly drives me to pursue good purposes and to be a better person. I hope they will be proud of their dad for this book.

I am incredibly indebted to my wife, Soohee. Without her love, encouragement, and advice, I could not achieve anything in my life. I have appreciated our journey, together with love, toward our shared goal and mission. I thank her for unconditionally supporting me to follow my vision and dreams.

Finally, I thank you, Jesus Christ, for everything you have done and will do for me. I can never repay to your love and sacrifice for me but will keep and follow your word for my whole life.

– Sunghan Ryu

Introduction

Picture the first immersive virtual reality (VR) headset,[1] a honey-harvesting beehive for home,[2] innovative online courseware for teaching coding to students,[3] a mystery-genre film production based on a terminated television series,[4] an inventive travel jacket with 15 features including a built-in neck pillow and earphone holders,[5] flower-decorated canes produced by a grandmother,[6] and a charity festival that started from potato salad.[7]

These imaginative and ingenious projects were initiated from entirely different grounds and stories, respectively, but have one special ingredient in common. They could happen in life thanks to crowdfunding, an initiative undertaken to raise money for a campaign of a creator, an entrepreneur, or an artist, ordinary people like us, by collecting small to medium amounts of funding from the public, mainly through an online platform.

The progress of information systems has expanded the scope of crowd participation in diverse business activities, including marketing campaigns, new product development, and societal activities, such as supporting social causes and community events. Recently, moreover, such participation has extended to fundraising, named crowdfunding. It serves to democratize the distribution of capital and the process of innovation, enabling creators from different domains in a way that could not be supported under traditional systems, such as banks and venture capitalists (VCs). Crowdfunding performs a role in connecting creators with novel ideas to contributors with diverse motivations to financially support campaigns. At the beginning phase of crowdfunding around 2010, there was a relatively small market of early adopters. The overall crowdfunding industry is on track to account for comparable total funding amounts with annual investment from the VC industry.[8] For example, as of October 2019, Kickstarter, a world-leading crowdfunding platform, has raised $4.5 billion from around 17 million people for more than 170,000 campaigns since its launch in 2009.[9] The major categories of the campaigns launched at Kickstarter include film, music, publishing, art, and technology.

The role of crowdfunding in democratization of capital

Historically, groups of expert investors were heavily involved in financing for creativity and innovation in their earlier stages. They used their own funds to invest in promising individuals and organizations. They nurtured them with valuable advice and readily available networks to help them grow their businesses. By its nature, this access to, and investment in, promising individuals and organizations was generally restricted to small groups of such experts. Regular individuals found it difficult to gain access to and participate in early-stage financing, even when they had the financial resources at hand. Those barriers have been lowered by the arrival of crowdfunding. Ordinary people have new access to financing and thus obtaining returns from those new creations and innovations.

From the other side, crowdfunding gives individuals and organizations another way to raise capital outside of the experts and turn to the crowd for their projects. They can promote their ideas to their (potential) fans, users, or customers. Crowdfunding is effective to create greater loyalty within networks. Crowdfunding expansion is good news for creators with new ideas across domains. Opening large opportunities for creators apart from the limited pool of financing channels gives them access to money like never before.

Specifically, in the business domain, innovative ventures in their early stages usually raised capital through VCs, but the number of ventures that receive investments from VCs is surprisingly low. For example, whereas VCs invested more than $84 billion in the US market in 2017, that capital was distributed across only 8,076 companies.[10] Considering that there are almost 6 million ventures in the United States, the portion of ventures that obtain VC investment is just a piece. Moreover, the majority of ventures that receive VC funding are usually located in big cities, such as San Francisco, Boston, and New York. These metro cities easily draw many entrepreneurial talents because infrastructure and systems are more favorable to those ventures and thus investors for managing portfolio ventures. Many VCs are performed in these cities, where networks are strong. This tendency indicates that a large part of the United States, outside these large cities, goes underfunded. Situations are similar across the world. Crowdfunding gives money-seeking ventures a way to sidestep VCs and obtain funding by another way. For the crowdfunding platforms, concentration in these top cities is surprisingly low as friction in transactions could diminish due to geographical distance.

More importantly, crowdfunding is playing roles for underfunded sectors neglected by institutional capital for a long time. For example, arts and cultural projects dominate crowdfunding. A majority of the campaigns on Kickstarter are related to creative sectors, as discussed. In many countries, crowdfunding now has more influence on the funding for new art projects than grants with expert judges.[11] Crowdfunding is leading a dramatic shift in how creativity is funded in recent years.

Among other inequalities in the capital market, gender bias is one of the most pervasive issues. Female entrepreneurs tend to launch ventures in sectors with relatively lower capital requirements and obtain remarkably smaller funding amounts from expert investors.[12] In 2016, ventures having female founders accounted for less than 5% of all VC investments.[13] The difference is even clearer on the investor side: Female investors make up only 26% of the angel investors and less than 6% of partners at VC firms.[14] Crowdfunding could play a role in fixing this gender bias. A strand of statistics shows women represent a major portion of project leadership in crowdfunding platforms such as Kickstarter and Indiegogo.[15] A more promising fact is that around half of the contributors to Kickstarter campaigns are women.

Although crowdfunding is still in its early stages, it is helping democratize the capital markets. Crowdfunding possesses potential and capabilities in addressing existing biases. The crowds, thanks to the Internet, are able to evaluate the attractiveness and feasibility of projects comparable to experts. Crowdfunding can help those located outside larger cities to connect with potential contributors, especially for those launching campaigns in creative sectors. Long-existing gender bias barriers have been undeniably lowered in crowdfunding platforms. Crowdfunding is playing a role in the democratization of creativity, innovation, and entrepreneurship.

Blooming creativity and innovation in the digital era

With the democratization of capital, crowdfunding is changing the landscapes of different sectors and domains where creativity and innovation are core components. Creativity and innovation are blooming due to crowdfunding as it generates solutions for some long-existing problems in the world of creativity and innovation.

Crowdfunding has dramatically expanded for creators in diverse domains to find funding, validate their ideas, build up new communities, and pursue their careers and businesses in the long term. Creators can gain meaningful benefits within their fields through crowdfunding. For some creators, it helps them secure funding for distributing the output from their projects. Other crowdfunding campaigns could lead to attention from important business partners. Another group of creators is delighted to have freedom from the external control of institutional sponsors for their work. New ventures and nonprofit organizations have their beginnings through crowdfunding. Moreover, many creators generate sustainable revenue from their projects after bringing them to life.[16]

Specifically, crowdfunding contributes to creativity and innovation in four dimensions.

Most of all, crowdfunding tackles the lack of financing channels, a long-running challenge in those domains. It is more effective than traditional financing channels in several aspects. Initiating a crowdfunding campaign on a platform is more productive in promoting an idea and message to potential contributors rather than applying for a bank loan and contacting accredited investors such as VCs. When crowdfunding works properly, it has an immediate impact on revenue. Successful crowdfunding offers creators a chance to focus on their work without being annoyed by pursuing external financing. Crowdfunding also enables them to compensate collaborators, who are creators as well. Those creative collaborators would not have been compensated otherwise.

Second, crowdfunding helps creators validate their creativity and innovation. When potential contributors, who will be turning to customers later, show interest in a creator's creativity and innovation, it generates evidence addressing that others believe in what they are creating. Moreover, crowdfunding platforms, such as Kickstarter, provide creators with handy digital technology tools for promoting communication flow between creators and contributors. On campaign pages, there are specific questions about the creativity and innovation that creators offer and the methods for bringing them to life. Creators obtain immediate response and feedback on whether their projects are meaningful and feasible. It is basically an opportunity for large-scale brainstorming or focus group interviews to refine ideas. Considering some great creativity and innovation undeniably come from important but unrealized value, it is important to seize any opportunity from contributor response and feedback in validating and refining ideas. In addition to validating ideas, creators can leverage crowdfunding to test their target markets. Crowdfunding offers creators an opportunity to analyze contributor conversion and engagement. Creators can examine how potential customers perceive their products, how close they are positioned to the right price range, and finally how it would generate performance in the market at later stages.

Third, crowdfunding creates a new supporting community for creators. Crowdfunding basically differs from other institutional financing channels in terms of whether the primary motivation for contribution is financial return. Contributors in the crowdfunding context may possess certain motivation for financial return. But, they are more likely to participate in crowdfunding campaigns with more diverse motivations, such as relationship building and supporting creators. In this regard, crowdfunding gains early adopters, turning to devoted advocates and consisting of a community for creators in later stages. Those are the people who believe in creativity and innovation of the creators. The community is an essential component to the success of any crowdfunding campaign and the momentum required during and after closing the campaign. It is most likely to share the creators' creativity and innovation to their friends and family and reach them through their social networks. Based on the process, creators can build social capital for their projects and themselves. This supporting community is a remarkably important asset for creators in pursuing their creativity and innovation in longer terms after the campaign ends.

Finally, crowdfunding offers creators an opportunity to secure creative independence. Crowdfunding affords creators the opportunity to bring their creativity and innovations to life without negotiating their dreams. They are not able to obtain creative independence with other financing channels as they mostly require giving up a part of independence in their work. This condition is undoubtedly essential for creators to take risks needed to accelerate creativity and innovation. In addition, media coverage through the crowdfunding platforms promotes campaigns more and thus increases awareness for creators and their work. Successful crowdfunding is a promising channel to capture interest from different stakeholders, and it can generate more opportunities for creators. For example, crowdfunding affects career advancement of creators. Successful crowdfunding practices could fuel creators to enjoy more earnings and career development. Relatedly, whereas some portions of crowdfunding campaigns are sole tryouts, such as publications, films, and performances, others become ongoing ventures and organizations that empower creators to pursue their work in a sustainable manner.

Motivation for this book

As we discussed in the previous sections, crowdfunding has addressed the limitations and biases that traditional sources of financing, such as banks and VCs, bear. Crowdfunding promotes the launching and scaling of creative and innovative projects from different sectors by providing networked platforms and handy digital tools.

Understanding crowdfunding is important for two reasons. First, from an academic perspective, it provides an opportunity to expand our knowledge on how participation of the customer (or crowd) in creative domains has evolved and what implications we could find from this advancement. Second, from a practical perspective, we could identify important roles of crowdfunding as an alternative financing channel for business and other practices in addition to fundraising itself.

While the limitation of the traditional capital market with its definite inequality has been discussed extensively, crowdfunding is expected to resolve the imbalance with a new approach and foster new ventures and organizations that have been neglected by conventional institutions. Crowdfunding promotes creativity and innovation, thereby supplying fuel for the sustainable development of our society.

In this regard, this book aims to expand our understanding on crowdfunding, focusing on whether crowdfunding contributes to our communities and society and, if so, how. More specifically, this book intends to explore what aspects of crowdfunding fuel creativity and innovation and have potential to improve our world. For addressing these issues, in addition to my own research and consulting projects on crowdfunding, for more than seven years from 2012 to 2019, I reviewed the extant literature of crowdfunding across different disciplines, for example, entrepreneurship, information systems, and marketing. I then connected those findings to the best crowdfunding practices, generating real changes to life. I was struck by the changes made through crowdfunding and started to believe in capabilities and the potential behind crowdfunding to improve, cultivate, and change the world in a slow but steady way. I then realized that there was no such book like this, which integrates the existing academic work with real practices in the domain for demonstrating the important roles of crowdfunding for the world.

The title of this book, *Beauty of Crowdfunding (BOC)*, and this book project were originated from these reflections. Presenting the most insightful and relevant academic studies and corresponding practices and cases with the highest level of clarity are my objectives with this book. By reading *BOC*, readers identify five beautiful aspects of crowdfunding—*creativity, diversity, balance, connection,* and *change*—and how those aspects affect creative, business, and social practices. I hope readers will clearly understand the findings and implications of *BOC*.

For clarification, although there are different types of crowdfunding (more details are discussed in Chapter 2), *BOC* mainly focuses on the reward-based crowdfunding model, where contributors support campaigns in exchange for rewards of diverse values, while shedding a little light on the equity-based crowdfunding model, where contributors select the preferred campaigns in exchange for stocks and other monetary incentives. The reward-based crowdfunding model is a good fit for diverse creators across domains, such as artists, musicians, filmmakers, inventors, and social enterprises. More importantly, whereas other types of crowdfunding models, including equity-based, are closely related to the existing sectors and limited to certain contexts, reward-based crowdfunding offers diverse intersections to creators for fueling creativity and innovation. In addition, findings from reward-based crowdfunding could potentially provide meaningful implications to those different types as each of them shares some similar aspects to reward-based crowdfunding, respectively.

What this book presents you

Although crowdfunding plays an increasing role in financing and promoting different projects across disciplines, including businesses, creative practices, and social movements, the extant literature on crowdfunding has myopically focused on tactical aspects such as success of campaigns inside crowdfunding platforms. Nevertheless, a perspective from the holistic point of view on what potential impact crowdfunding has on our community and society has been lacking. We only fragmentally understand how crowdfunding generates differences and do not know about the potential role of crowdfunding in democratization of capital and blooming creativity and innovation. Moreover, the linkage between academic findings from the pioneering literature and best practices in the industry is rather weak, and thus implications for both parties are limited. I expect readers to find this book project a comprehensive guide for understanding the crowdfunding phenomenon based on both research and practice. I strongly believe that this book can also serve as a bridge linking academicians to practitioners in the domain.

In this regard, *BOC* is intended to aid three different but interrelated reader groups.

First, it aims to provide knowledge on status-quo crowdfunding research from a systematic view and thus call for promising future research on crowdfunding to academic researchers, particularly in information systems, management, economics, and entrepreneurship domains. I expect them to gain benefits from *BOC* by figuring out what aspects of crowdfunding have been addressed by academic research so far and being exposed to some provoking crowdfunding cases in practice.

More broadly, industry experts and professionals should learn new knowledge from *BOC* as it suggests why and how crowdfunding influences related domains, such as cultural and creative areas, technology sectors, and society as a whole. They will be able to develop better understanding of recent crowdfunding phenomenon based on findings from advanced research and best practices. Moreover, the implications in this book, drawn from research and case studies, will help current and potential entrepreneurs, investors, marketers, and policy officers understand the important roles of crowdfunding in the digital age.

Finally, as *BOC* is essentially a book about societal changes through collective actions of (ordinary) people aided by technological advancement, if anyone wants to understand how those combinations potentially improve our world to a better place, this book is for them. Democratization of capital is a starting point. Crowdfunding would open up a series of different doors to new changes in the future.

Outline of chapters

Part 1

The chapters in Part 1 of the book present some basic notions of crowdfunding. From Part 1, readers will learn the basic concepts of crowdfunding and related knowledge around crowdfunding, helping them understand the remaining parts.

In Chapter 1, I lay out a series of "crowdfunded" projects in history, including the stories of Alexander Pope, Mozart, and the Statue of Liberty, and demonstrate what aspects distinguish crowdfunding today from those historical practices.

In Chapter 2, I brief the essential components of crowdfunding and how it works with three main players: creator, contributor, and platform operator. In addition, four different types of crowdfunding models, including donation based, lending based, reward based, and equity based, and their differences are summarized.

A complicated nature of crowdfunding required review of broader spectrums of the literature. In Chapter 3, I review the literature on social human nature, including crowd behavior and cooperative behavior. Studies are then thoroughly examined on two essential monetary behaviors of people: donation and investment. Relatedly, some antecedents of crowdfunding, such as VC, customer participation, and crowd participation are discussed.

In Chapter 4, I review the previous literature on crowdfunding, regarding factors affecting the success of crowdfunding campaigns and individual contributors' funding behavior, and implications from the findings. The chapter provides some guidelines, based on the literature, for potential creators and demonstrates future research directions.

Part 2

The chapters in Part 2 are organized with the five beautiful aspects of crowdfunding behind the phenomenon. Each chapter in the part will take readers to related academic research, corresponding practices, and key takeaways.

8 Introduction

Chapter 5 focuses on creativity, the most dominant virtue of crowdfunding. Crowdfunding helps and promotes the bloom of creativity in different aspects by solving financial shortage and generating ideas from the crowd. When seeing the campaign categories of crowdfunding platform, for example, Kickstarter and Indiegogo, we can find the major parts of campaigns are related to creative and cultural domains. Moreover, those creative crowdfunding campaigns tend to be more appreciated by contributors at the platforms. Some key examples include the following:

- Kickstarter and Sundance Film Festivals: In six years, from 2011 to 2017, 106 films have played at the Sundance Film Festival that have been crowdfunded at Kickstarter, and more than 430 Sundance alumni have run Kickstarter campaigns.
- Patreon, a membership-based crowdfunding platform founded in 2013, provides artists and creators with handy tools to operate subscription-based content creation. It supports them to obtain funding directly from their patrons (supporters) on a regular basis or per creative project. It is popular among diverse categories of creators who post regularly online.

Chapter 6 addresses the diversity of crowdfunding. In the crowdfunding context, different types of creators and contributors exist. The most successful crowdfunding campaigns include products and services from different domains, such as Smart Watch, Game, Icebox, Travel Jacket, Video Game Console, Backpack, and so on. When it comes to small to medium-sized campaigns, everything can happen in crowdfunding platforms. For example, a Kickstarter campaign was launched by a grandson for producing a stylish cane for his grandma. Creators and contributors participate in crowdfunding with diverse motivations and thus behave in different ways. Based on my own research projects, I introduce different types of creators and contributors based on their motivations to participate in crowdfunding.

Chapter 7 supports the role of crowdfunding as a step toward democratization of capital. Crowdfunding sheds light to the domains that have been neglected by legitimate institutions, for example, banks and VCs, and offer benefits to those with disadvantages in location, product type, gender, and so on. Traditional capital market is geographic dependent as the major portion of players are located in a few clusters, but crowdfunding addresses bias through an online platform and opening opportunities to the public. Traditional capitals also prefer certain types of industries and products, for example, software and technology-driven products. Crowdfunding is more favorable to and even prefers hardware products. Gender inequality in the capital market is a huge obstacle. Crowdfunding has the potential to solve these inequality problems.

Chapter 8 deals with connection, enabled by crowdfunding. Crowdfunding builds up new community not only for fundraising but also for new connections, generating more value than pure monetary returns. Successful crowdfunding campaigns validate market demand, but more importantly it builds a supporting community.[17] A software engineer named Zach Brown launched a crowdfunding campaign to raise $10 on Kickstarter to make a potato salad. However, this small online joke turned to online viral sensation, and he obtained $55,000 from about 7,000 contributors. He used all the extra funding to launch a festival for a charity in his town. It was started for fun at first, but turned into a new community. At the end of the chapter, based on the recommendations from the platform operators and successful creators, I list essential action plans for building a community even before the launch of a campaign.

Chapter 9 focuses on whether crowdfunding has a power to change the world. Market trends and representative practices show that crowdfunding has the potential to change the world into a better place as many important but neglected things can be crowdfunded. Social enterprise, scientific research, and journalism are remarkable examples. Social enterprises stand at a disadvantage, relative to commercial enterprises, in acquiring funds through traditional financial institutions, even though there is an all-time high interest in social enterprises. Crowdfunding has emerged to address the needs of social enterprises with limited access to traditional capital. With lack of funding for discovering new scientific knowledge, any scientist can run a campaign to raise funds for a research project. For example, Experiment, founded in 2012, is one of the biggest crowdfunding platforms for scientific research. Crowdfunded journalism financially supports independent journalism with funding from the general public. The potential contributor can judge and support the work of journalists launched in the crowdfunding platforms. Crowdfunded journalism is a bold movement in the face of giant media companies that seek to control public opinion. It is effective to promote public engagement and spread those important issues. Finally, I demonstrate the potential of civic crowdfunding based on the Crowdfund London case.

Part 3

Chapter 10 presents some key challenges and potential drawbacks of crowdfunding. Crowdfunding is not an easy task as many creators assume. Fulfillment of the contributors, detecting fraud, and protection of ideas are examples of key challenges in crowdfunding practices. For example, according to a survey on Kickstarter creators, among funded campaigns, a failure to deliver accounts for around 9% of all projects.[18] I also deal with the dark side of crowdfunding, which limits its potential to perform as a change maker. The chapter offers possible resolutions for those challenges based on some of the best practices and advice from academics and platform operators.

Chapter 11, the last chapter of *BOC*, introduces a perspective on post-campaign performance of crowdfunding success. Even though crowdfunding plays an increasing role in the venture finance, the extant literature on crowdfunding has myopically focused on the success of campaigns inside crowdfunding platforms. Nevertheless, we still know little about how crowdfunding can influence the whole structure of the venture financing industry. This chapter

10 *Introduction*

demonstrates effects of crowdfunding success on subsequent performance from the different perspectives.

Finally, in the epilogue, I offer my views on the future of crowdfunding. As the crowdfunding market grows bigger, we will see the divergence between platforms for scaled businesses and those for smaller campaigns become more explicit. On the one hand, equity-based crowdfunding platforms, like CrowdCube and CircleUp, and some related platforms provide a clear offering for business fundraising and investing. On the other hand, crowdfunding will be increasingly atomized, with niche platforms serving specific domains of interest. For example, Seed&Spark, designed specifically for filmmakers, combines a subscription-based crowdfunding model with a streaming service. Betabrand operates as a crowdfunded retail service for supporting fashion designers. Crowdfunding will also expand by converging with different players, domains, and technologies.

Notes

1. www.kickstarter.com/projects/1523379957/oculus-rift-step-into-the-game
2. www.indiegogo.com/projects/flow-hive-honey-on-tap-directly-from-your-beehive#/
3. www.indiegogo.com/projects/an-hour-of-code-for-every-student#/
4. www.kickstarter.com/projects/559914737/the-veronica-mars-movie-project
5. www.kickstarter.com/projects/baubax/the-worlds-best-travel-jacket-with-15-features-bau
6. www.kickstarter.com/projects/998024426/happy-canes-spring-13-canes-for-grandma
7. www.kickstarter.com/projects/zackdangerbrown/potato-salad
8. https://medium.com/startup-grind/trends-show-crowdfunding-to-surpass-vc-in-2016-65df924d8a82
9. www.kickstarter.com/help/stats
10. www.forbes.com/sites/howardmarks/2018/06/10/how-crowdfunding-is-disrupting-vcs/
11. https://cmr.berkeley.edu/browse/articles/58_2/5812/
12. https://cmr.berkeley.edu/browse/articles/58_2/5812/
13. www.forbes.com/sites/howardmarks/2018/06/10/how-crowdfunding-is-disrupting-vcs/
14. https://cmr.berkeley.edu/browse/articles/58_2/5812/
15. www.theatlantic.com/business/archive/2014/08/women-are-more-likely-to-secure-kickstarter-funding-than-men/376081/
16. www.kickstarter.com/blog/kickstarters-impact-on-the-creative-economy
17. www.crowdfundinsider.com/2016/04/84639-ethan-mollick-the-value-of-crowdfunding-is-community/
18. www.kickstarter.com/fulfillment

Part 1
About crowdfunding

1 Crowdfunding
An old story?

For centuries, creators experimented with a model collecting certain amounts of money from their patrons to pursue their new work, which is basically identical to the crowdfunding model today. In 1713, Alexander Pope, a famous 18th-century English poet and writer, set out to translate 15,693 lines of Homer's *Iliad*, an honored ancient Greek poem, into English.[1] Pope went through the crowdfunding model for launching this project. He crafted his pitch for attracting potential patrons for his project, saying: "This work shall be printed in six volumes in quarto, on the finest paper, and on a letter new cast on purpose; with ornaments and initial letters engraved on copper."[2] In return for appreciation in the acknowledgments and receiving the first edition of the book, 750 patrons pledged two gold guineas to sponsor his project even before he put a pen to it. It took five long years to finish the six volumes, but the reward was worth waiting: the greatest translation of Homer's *Iliad* in English that has survived until to today.[3,4] The patrons were listed in an early edition of the book, and it was presented to them as a reward. In addition, they might enjoy the pleasure of participating in the task of bringing a new creative work into the world. For himself, Pope could establish his absolute competitiveness among the talents of his time.

The crowdfunding model was also used in music as far back as the 18th century. In 1783, after a few years, Mozart picked a similar path as Pope.[5] He had a plan to perform three new pieces of piano concertos at a concert hall in Vienna. He distributed an invitation to prospective patrons offering an earlier version of manuscripts to those who pledged – basically the same way that crowdfunding campaigns today offer contributors the chance to get the output into their hands first: "These three concertos, which can be performed with full orchestra including wind instruments, or only a quattro, that is with 2 violins, 1 viola and violoncello, will be available at the beginning of April to those who have subscribed for them."[6,7] Interestingly, like many crowdfunding campaigns today, Mozart failed on his first attempt to collect enough funding for his project. One year later he attempted again, and 176 patrons pledged enough funding to make it possible for his concertos to be performed. In addition to Mozart, Beethoven also relied upon the support of patrons for creating new pieces, for whom he provided private performances and earlier copies of works they commissioned for an exclusive period prior to their official publication.

14 About crowdfunding

Another early example of crowdfunding model can be found in one of the world's most famous landmarks: the Statue of Liberty in New York.[8] The Statue of Liberty was designed by French sculptor Frederic Auguste Bartholdi and financially supported by the government of France as a diplomatic gift to the United States. In 1875, due to the postwar vulnerability in France, a French politician, Édouard René de Laboulaye, proposed that the French government finance production of the statue and the United States provide the site, build the podium, and assemble pieces of the statue. By 1885, the Statue of Liberty arrived in New York in pieces, but the United States, specifically the New York government, had been unable to finance the budget for the podium and assembly of the statue. A committee named the American Committee of the Statue of Liberty was in charge of fundraising but fell apart, and New York Governor Grover Cleveland turned down using city funds to pay for it. Congress thus could not agree on a funding composition. Amid this unpredictability, other big cities, such as Boston, San Francisco, and Philadelphia, offered to settle the money for the podium in return for its relocation. New York had no feasible alternative before renowned publisher Joseph Pulitzer launched a fundraising campaign for raising $100,000 to support the project in his newspaper *The New York World (The World)*. He promised to print the name of every contributor in *The World*, no matter how much amount of the money given. In five months *The World* raised $101,091 from more than 160,000 people, most of whom contributed less than a dollar.[9] The statue could be finally dedicated on October 28, 1886.

Those projects from the old days would be representative crowdfunding campaigns among those initiated at Kickstarter if launched today. Basically, similar to the crowdfunding model, for certain projects with clear purpose, they raised money from a large pool of people; each pledged small to medium amounts of money. So, is crowdfunding today a replication of these old stories? Although there are undeniable overlaps between then and now, the crowdfunding model is essentially different from those classical practices in three aspects.

First, the internet makes the campaigns dramatically more visible and accessible to all. Most information about the projects is presented through campaign pages on crowdfunding platforms and can be shared via the web in a seamless manner. Any person can participate in supporting any campaign at minimum cost for access and transaction. More importantly, potential contributors can see the level of support from other people as well as its timing before making their own funding decisions, generating more dynamics in the crowdfunding context.

Second, relatedly to the first aspect, crowdfunding has opened up new tremendous opportunities for creators with different backgrounds, which would not have been available before the internet era. Thanks to the connected world, creators, including ordinary people with favorable ideas, can reach a circle of people who want to help each other bring creative and imaginative ideas to life. Pope, Mozart, and Pulitzer were already preeminent figures in their time before launching their own projects for raising money. Although those practices were allowed only for someone with strong profile and background in the pre-internet era, what is happening today is widening the gates for everyone who wants to expand their creativity (even for fun in some cases).

Last, crowdfunding offers something unique other funding channels do not – a way to distribute and commercialize creativity. Through a crowdfunding campaign, individual creators can tab to a community of contributors. This community may perform as supporters, beta testers, early customers, and enthusiastic fans. Crowdfunding today is much more than a simple financing mechanism that has the potential to change the landscapes of several important domains, including but not limited to production, financing, distribution, and marketing.

Although crowdfunding is still a rapidly emerging and evolving phenomenon, this book intends to highlight the changes made through crowdfunding as it exists today and the potential impacts of this phenomenon on our communities and society.

Notes

1 www.kickstarter.com/blog/kickstarter-before-kickstarter
2 http://rbscp.lib.rochester.edu/3948
3 www.nytimes.com/1997/06/01/books/on-reading-pope-s-homer.html
4 www.kickstarter.com/blog/kickstarter-before-kickstarter
5 www.virgin.com/entrepreneur/brief-history-crowdfunding
6 www.kickstarter.com/blog/kickstarter-before-kickstarter
7 www.hyperion-records.co.uk/dc.asp?dc=D_CDH55333
8 www.bbc.com/news/magazine-21932675
9 www.virgin.com/entrepreneur/brief-history-crowdfunding

2 How crowdfunding works

Some core aspects of crowdfunding

We can find a set of definitions of crowdfunding from the previous literature. Part of the earliest literature is presented as follows:

- A collective effort by people who network and pool their money together, usually via the internet, to invest in and support efforts initiated by other people or organizations (Ordanini et al., 2011)
- Tapping a large, dispersed audience, dubbed as "the crowd," for small sums of money to fund a project or a venture (Lehner, 2012)
- An open call over the internet for financial resources in the form of a monetary donation, sometimes in exchange for a future product, service, or reward (Gerber et al., 2012)
- An open call, essentially through the internet, for the provision of financial resources either in the form of donation or in exchange for some form of reward and/or voting rights to support initiatives for specific purposes (Belleflamme et al., 2014)
- The efforts by entrepreneurial individuals and groups – cultural, social, and for profit – to fund their ventures by drawing on relatively small contributions from a relatively large number of individuals using the internet, without standard financial intermediaries (Mollick, 2014)

There are evident common aspects across those definitions. First, crowdfunding is an initiative for fundraising. It is apparently a new type of financing approach using new channels. Second, it is conducted for a campaign of a creator. The scope of creators in the crowdfunding context is broader, including but not limited to entrepreneurs, artists, and social enterprises. Third, it raises money by collecting small to medium amounts of funding from the crowd, basically consisting of the undisclosed public. This aspect is the most distinctive characteristic of crowdfunding, distinguishing it from the existing financing models, such as VC and business angles. Finally, all transactions and communication between the creator and the crowds are managed mainly through the online platform.

From this notion of crowdfunding, we could identify that three main players are engaged in crowdfunding. The first player is the creator, who creates new campaigns and seeks funding from the crowds. The crowds constitute the second player, contributors.[1] Contributors decide whether to support the campaigns or not after considering an expected compensation from the campaigns, including intrinsic values (e.g., altruism, fun) and extrinsic benefits (e.g., rewards, relationship). The third player is the platform operator, which brings the other two players on board and provides an opportunity for exchanging values.

Most crowdfunding platforms have four common properties that are essential for enabling and promoting the transactions between two players: They are 1) a standardized format for creators to pitch their campaigns, 2) a payment system allowing a large volume of small financial transactions, 3) a display of funding progress, and 4) tools for creators and contributors to communicate with each other.

Once a creator uploads some mandatory information introducing the campaign (e.g., goal amount, funding duration, planned rewards in return for funding), and after the platform operator confirms the appropriateness of the campaign and the fulfillment of the requirements, the campaign page goes live on the crowdfunding platform. Potential contributors are exposed to the page and decide whether to pledge to the campaign before the due date, which is set by the creator. If a contributor decides to pledge for the campaign, a transaction between the contributor and the platform takes place. The record of this transaction is reflected on the campaign page as an aggregated form, including total funding amount and number of contributors to date. If the funding amount reaches (or exceeds) the goal within the designated period, the platform operator will transfer the collected money to the creator after deducting brokerage, usually 5–10% of the total amount. After the transmission, the creator fulfills the duties of developing the campaign and delivering rewards to contributors as proposed. In the case of funding failure, on the other hand, the platform operator typically cancels all the transactions, indicating that there will be no financial loss to the contributors. Some crowdfunding platforms allow creators to keep all funds regardless of reaching the goal amount, but the major platforms still transmit the funds raised to creators only if they meet the goal amount.

The whole crowdfunding process is represented in Figure 2.1.

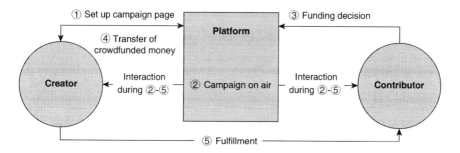

Figure 2.1 Crowdfunding process

Crowdfunding as a two-sided platform

The two-sided platform (TSP) is a marketplace that enables direct transactions between two distinct types of affiliated customer groups between which cross-network externalities exist. Although the TSP is a tool for facilitating transactions (Eisenmann et al., 2006; Hagiu and Wright, 2015), it cannot control the transactions between the two sides by itself (Rochet and Tirole, 2003; Rochet and Tirole, 2006). Additionally, the roles of two different participants are distinguishable at the transaction point (Hagiu and Wright, 2015), and each customer group is affiliated to the TSP. Finally, the size and quality of one side affect its ability to draw users on the other side (Wright, 2004; Evans, 2003; Bakos and Katsamakas, 2008). Hagiu and Wright (2015) compared the TSP to resellers and input suppliers. Resellers are different from TSPs because they lack direct interaction between the two user groups. Input suppliers are distinguishable from TSPs because only one user group is affiliated with the platform, whereas the other has no direct relationship with it.

This has been one of the most actively studied research themes in diverse disciplines, including economics, information systems, and strategy and marketing. Practitioners are also interested in the TSP because of its importance and influence on the market, driven by the advent of remarkable services such as Apple's app store and eBay. Prior studies have attempted to understand the nature and mechanism of the TSP, focusing on economic aspects such as price structure and policy issues (Evans, 2003; Wright, 2004; Parker and Van Alstyne, 2005; Rochet and Tirole, 2006).

From the notions of TSP, we can conclude that the crowdfunding (platform) is a representative example of the TSP. The crowdfunding platform itself cannot control transactions between creators and contributors but provides communication tools and payment systems that facilitate transactions. Further, both creators and contributors are affiliated with the crowdfunding platform. Another important point is the existence of a clear and strong cross-network externality between the creators and contributors. The size and quality of one side significantly affects the attraction of users to the other side.

Different types of crowdfunding

Four types of crowdfunding models are commonly discussed depending on the characteristics of funding returns. These four models are donation based, lending based, reward based, and equity based in order of debut to the world.

Donation-based crowdfunding is designed for charities and those who raise money for social causes or personal purposes to gather donations online and to enable them to support the campaign. Contributors usually donate their money without (or with relatively low) expectation for certain returns from their contribution. Although most established charity organizations may coordinate the crowdfunding process through their own websites, crowdfunding platforms can be useful for smaller organizations and individuals. GoFundMe[2] and Kiva[3] are representative examples of donation-based crowdfunding platforms.

Lending-based crowdfunding provides contributors with the chance to fund a project in return for financial interest. This type of crowdfunding may provide creators with financing the funds at a lower cost than a bank loan. It may work best for ventures with a track record of business. LendingClub[4] and Prosper[5] are typical examples of the lending-based crowdfunding platform.

Reward-based crowdfunding allows contributors to support a creator's campaign in return for nonmonetary benefits. This type of crowdfunding is specifically useful for creative projects and ventures with new product ideas. In this model, the more contributors pledge to the campaign, the greater rewards they can receive. Kickstarter[6] and Indiegogo[7] are representative players for reward-based crowdfunding.

Finally, in the equity-based crowdfunding, contributors will support a campaign in return for shares or a small stake in its business or venture. This type of crowdfunding may work best for growing companies in domains where there is high potential for growth and thus return. CrowdCube[8] and CircleUp[9] are leading platforms in the equity-based crowdfunding domain.

Notes

1 They are named in different ways according to situations. Some examples include backers, donors, crowdfunders, sponsors, patrons, and supporters.
2 www.gofundme.com
3 www.kiva.org
4 www.lendingclub.com
5 www.prosper.com
6 www.kickstarter.com
7 www.indiegogo.com
8 www.crowdcube.com
9 www.circleup.com

References

Bakos, Y. & Katsamakas, E. 2008. Design and Ownership of Two-Sided Networks: Implications for Internet Platforms. *Journal of Management Information Systems*, 25, 171–202.

Belleflamme, P., Lambert, T. & Schwienbacher, A. 2014. Crowdfunding: Tapping the Right Crowd. *Journal of Business Venturing*, 29, 585–609.

Eisenmann, T., Parker, G. & Van Alstyne, M. W. 2006. Strategies for Two-Sided Markets. *Harvard Business Review*, 84, 92–102.

Evans, D. S. 2003. Some Empirical Aspects of Multi-Sided Platform Industries. *Review of Network Economics*, 2, 191–209.

Gerber, E. M., Hui, J. S. & Kuo, P. 2012. Crowdfunding: Why People Are Motivated to Post and Fund Projects on Crowdfunding Platforms. *Proceedings of the International Workshop on Design, Influence, and Social Technologies: Techniques, Impacts and Ethics*, Northwestern University, Evanston, IL. Retrieved on March.

Hagiu, A. & Wright, J. (2015). Multi-sided platforms. *International Journal of Industrial Organization*, 43, 162–174.

Lehner, O. 2012. A Literature Review and Research Agenda for Crowdfunding of Social Ventures. *Research Colloquium on Social Entrepreneurship*, 16–19 July, University of Oxford, Skoll Center of SAID Business School.

Mollick, E. 2014. The Dynamics of Crowdfunding: An Exploratory Study. *Journal of Business Venturing*, 29, 1–16.

Ordanini, A., Miceli, L., Pizzetti, M. & Parasuraman, A. 2011. Crowd-Funding: Transforming Customers into Investors through Innovative Service Platforms. *Journal of Service Management*, 22, 443–470.

Parker, G. G. & Van Alstyne, M. W. 2005. Two-Sided Network Effects: A Theory of Information Product Design. *Management Science*, 51, 1494–1504.

Rochet, J. C. & Tirole, J. 2003. Platform Competition in Two-Sided Markets. *Journal of the European Economic Association*, 1, 990–1029.

Rochet, J. C. & Tirole, J. 2006. Two-Sided Markets: A Progress Report. *The RAND Journal of Economics*, 37, 645–667.

Wright, J. 2004. One-Sided Logic in Two-Sided Markets. *Review of Network Economics*, 3, 1–21.

3 Understanding the foundation of crowdfunding

The complicated nature of crowdfunding required review of levels and spectrums of the literature. I start from literature on social human nature, including crowd behavior and cooperative behavior. Studies were then thoroughly examined on two essential monetary behaviors of people: donation and investment. Finally, the literature on some precedents of crowdfunding, such as VCs, customer participation, and crowd participation, are discussed.

Collective human behavior

Crowd behavior

Classical crowd behavior theories are based on the main idea of Gustav Le Bon. He claimed that people who are in a crowd differ from those who are not because the anonymity formed by the crowd allows people to lose intense concern for public opinion of their actions. The Contagion Theory describes large numbers of people forsaking personal responsibility and giving up themselves to the spreading emotions of the crowd (Le Bon, 1897).

Deindividuation Theory proposes the concept of diminishing the sense of individuality in crowd behavior (Zimbardo, 1969). Environmental conditions such as anonymity or close group unity lowered self-awareness of an individual in the crowd. They induce "deindividuation symptoms" including the weakened constraints against impulsive behaviors (Zimbardo, 1969; Jaffe and Yinon, 1979). However, the hypotheses of Deindividuation Theory are limited because the notion of deindividuation is circumstantial. Furthermore, it is explored that crowds frequently behave in a composed manner and even prosocial ways.

Emergent-Norm Theory asserts that people in crowds make their own rules as they act (Turner and Killian, 1957). Due to the absence of preexisting norms, a distinctive behavior is perceived as an implicit norm, and inaction of the majority caused by normative pressures is interpreted as confirmation, which results in a collective behavior. However, the theory cannot generate persuasive explanations in the cases in which crowds gather for a specific purpose and behave logically.

As a counterargument against classical theories, Social Identity Theory (Reicher et al., 1995; Reicher, 1984) insists the social identity of the crowd provides norms for behavior, which indicates that individuals come together as members of a specific social group with a specific purpose. As the integration of two opposite approaches, the Social Identity Model of Deindividuation Effects (Reicher et al., 1995; Lea and Spears, 1991) has identified that the anonymity affects the relative salience of personality, compared to social identity of the crowd. The anonymity changes the personality of an individual, which is different from the social identity of the crowd, and the change results in the individual's conformity to group norms.

Cooperative behavior

Diverse research domains has suggested explanations for cooperative behaviors of human beings. In the perspective of evolutionary biology, the Theory of Group Selection proposed by Charles Darwin and developed by Wynne-Edwards (1962) indicates an individual could cooperate with similar others because "natural selection" is not operated in individual levels but among groups of organisms. Genetic Kinship Theory (Hamilton, 1964) has enhanced this approach by exploring that an individual favors the reproductive success of its relatives. In contrast to those "organism-centered" viewpoints adopted conventionally by scholars, Gene Selection Theory (Dawkins, 1976) suggests cooperation occurs through the differential survival of competing genes. A "selfish gene" produces altruism for organisms carrying it because the possibility of selection increases when those traits dominate.

From a different point of view, Trivers (1971) insisted the concept of "reciprocal altruism," in which an organism helps others with the expectation that they will act similarly at a later time. When "reciprocal altruism" cannot be applied, indicating no expectation for delayed reciprocity, Costly Signaling Theory (Hawkes, 1991) can be a good alternative. Individuals may often choose to engage in responsible behavior to heighten their image and status (Barclay and Willer, 2007).

Game Theory is the representative proposition for understanding cooperation among individuals in the perspective of economics (Leonard, 1995). The theory proposes analytical models of competition and cooperation among rational decision makers. Game Theory also notes that non-zero-sum games can potentially lead to cooperation (Scodel et al., 1959). In another viewpoint, Noë and Hammerstein (1994) suggested the concept of biological "market effect," which implies each individual in a society can benefit from specializing in one specific resource and acquiring other resources by cooperation as a way of trade.

From a perspective of sociology, Role Theory (Montgomery, 1998) regards an individual as a collection of social roles and asserts he/she helps others for the appropriate rule for interaction, regardless of the future relationship, whereas Norm Theory (Coleman, 1990) explains cooperation as the "norm" supported by authority and derived from the consensus of the society.

Human behavior in the monetary contexts

Investor behavior

Classical finance theories assume investors act rationally and consider all available information in the decision-making process.[1] They thus assume that investment markets are efficient, reflecting all available information in stock prices (i.e., Market Portfolio Theory, Markowitz, 1952; Capital Asset Pricing Model, Sharpe, 1964). Due to unrealistic assumptions of classical theories, however, behavioral finance which investigates choice of "normal investors" under uncertainty has drawn interest from academic and practical areas.

Nagy and Obenberger (1994) proposed the major frames of behavioral finance in Prospect Theory, such as "regret aversion" and "self-control." Prospect Theory suggests that people react differently to equivalent possibility depending on whether it is in the context of a gain or a loss (Kahneman and Tversky, 1979). In the context of a gain, for example, people tend to avoid risk (Tversky and Kahneman, 1974). Regret aversion, in this context, refers to the emotional reaction people experience after identifying their misjudgments. To avert regret, people pursue the conventional wisdom and invest in stocks that everyone else chooses. Self-control explains the propensity of some people to control emotions for delayed gratifications. For example, researchers found some investors valued dividends more than others (Shefrin and Statman, 1984; Thaler and Shefrin, 1981).

In addition to those frames, researchers investigated diverse heuristic decision processes of investors under uncertainty (Tversky and Kahneman, 1974). For example, "anchoring" refers to the tendency of investors making judgments by beginning at their own reference points and then adjusting imperfectly to reach a final decision. Similarly, "availability heuristic" is adopted to evaluate the possibility of an event on the basis of examples easily brought to mind. In another perspective, Alpert and Raiffa (1982) verified investors' propensity of "overconfidence." They found people usually overestimate their accuracy of knowledge. People are also overconfident about their positive outcomes in the past and recall more their successes than failures.

Finally, based on those frames and propositions, several empirical studies provide other evidence for understanding investor behavior. The results of a set of studies indicate individual characteristics such as gender, social characteristics, and past experience affect behaviors of an individual investor. For example, men choose riskier portfolios more than women (Sunden and Surette, 1998; Barber and Odean, 2001), and social investors are more likely to invest in the stock market compared to nonsocial investors (Hong et al., 2004). Intense experience in the past (e.g., Great Depression) also has a significant effect on individual investment choice (Malmendier and Nagel, 2011). In addition, personality (Filbeck et al., 2005), age (Wang and Hanna, 1997), peer effect (Brown et al., 2008), and income level (Grable, 2000; Riley Jr and Chow, 1992) are found to be associated with risk tolerance propensity, which directly affects the investment decisions.

Donor behavior

Research on charitable behavior is another literature stream that reflects the element of monetary decision-making (Guy and Patton, 1989). Sojka (1986) proposed the continuum of donor behavior classified into four categories: altruism, social conscious behavior, social status behavior, and non-altruism.

An altruistic motive for donating to charity is "a desire to cause social change, a warm glow, empathy, sympathy, pity, fear, and guilt" (Merchant and Ford, 2008). Conspicuous compassion is associated with feeling good, not doing good (Grace and Griffin, 2009; West, 2004). Social status motives refer to self-esteem, recognition, prestige, respect in the community, and peer pressure (Merchant and Ford, 2008). A non-altruistic motive comprises two different aspects. On one hand, it has an intrinsic aspect that implies the donor participates in charitable behaviors to maximize his/her satisfaction (Sherry Jr, 1983). On the other hand, the donor can be extrinsically motivated by economic benefits such as tax refunds (Lu Hsu et al., 2005).

In addition to those classifications, Shier and Handy (2012) suggested two primary indicators of donation: the capacity and the inclination. The capacity indicates a donor's financial resources, whereas the inclination means the social and psychological propensity of a person toward charitable giving.

A strand of empirical studies verifies who donates and why they do. They show age (Kottasz, 2004; Grace and Griffin, 2006), gender (Lee and Chang, 2007; Micklewright and Schnepf, 2009; Pessemier et al., 1977), income (Radley and Kennedy, 1995; Bekkers, 2010; Bekkers, 2006), and social status (Micklewright and Schnepf, 2009) have considerable meaning for the prediction of donor behavior. The literature consistently shows age, being female, and high levels of education are positive characteristics for charitable giving. In terms of income level, the result shows financial capital promotes philanthropic behaviors, and donors with low income levels are motivated by empathy, whereas richer donors consider causing social changes.

Other aspects such as physical distance between the donor and the recipients (Bekkers and Schuyt, 2008), perceived accountability of the organization (Berman and Davidson, 2003), reputation of the organization (Handy, 2000), and performance of the organization (Sargeant et al., 2008) also showed significant impacts on donor behavior.

In the online context, Shier and Handy (2012) examined the importance of website design and accessibility, perceived credibility of the organization, and influence from others. And, Bennett (2009) found the factors affect impulsive donation decisions while browsing charity websites. In the study, emotive elements of the website, philanthropic characteristics of donors, and attractions for encouraging participation are identified as the main determinants of impulsive giving.

Some origins of crowdfunding

Venture capital

VCs are distinguished from other traditional financial institutions, such as banks, in terms of the characteristics of the firms they finance. Those firms record relatively high growth, high risk, and high return (Ueda, 2004). Once a VC fund is raised, the VCs must identify investment opportunities. VCs structure and execute deals with entrepreneurial teams and monitor investments. Ultimately, they are required to achieve some return on their capital (Sahlman, 1990). Fried and Hisrich (1994) developed the six-stage decision-making model of VC investment. They showed different activities occur in each stage (i.e., origination, VC firm-specific screen, generic screen, first-phase evaluations, second-phase evaluation, and closing). After funding is closed successfully, VCs perform services for those funded ventures, called portfolio companies. The services include aid to raise additional funds, strategic planning, and recruitment of management teams (Gorman and Sahlman, 1989).

Zider (1998) described the ideal entrepreneur in the perspective of VCs, such as "tells a compelling story and is presentable to outside investors" and "has realistic expectations about process and output." Hisrich and Jankowicz (1990) identified the three basic criteria for VC investments: concept (i.e., potential for growth, business idea, competitive advantage, and capital requirement), management (i.e., personal integrity, experience, and leadership), and returns (i.e., exit opportunity, a high rate of return, and a high absolute return). Other studies on VC investments also suggest important key criteria. They include fit with the VC, attractiveness of the industry, risks to be managed, previous experience in the industry, and a deep knowledge of the product (Riquelme and Rickards, 1992; Hall and Hofer, 1993; Macmillan et al., 1985).

Relational aspects are another critical indicator for VC investments. For example, business proposals previously reviewed by other VCs whom are trusted by the VC received a high degree of interest (Hall and Hofer, 1993). Another study shows that trust among nations significantly affects international investment decisions (Bottazzi et al., 2016). Through social network analysis, Hsu (2007) identified that previous founding experience and the ability of founding members to recruit management teams via their own network are positively associated with VC funding via direct tie and higher-venture valuation. Moreover, syndication or networking among VCs allows sharing of knowledge to make a decision of investing in risky ventures (Lerner, 1994; Bygrave, 1987).

Customer participation

The role of customers in business activity is one of the most attractive research interests in diverse areas, including marketing, strategy, and information system.

Lead User Theory has developed the concept of special customers' participation in improving existing products and services or developing new ones (Von Hippel, 1986; Urban and Von Hippel, 1988; Von Hippel and Katz, 2002). Those customers, who are called "lead users," are distinguished from other customers in two characteristics (Von Hippel, 1986; Franke et al., 2006). They are expected to obtain relatively high benefits from an innovation to their needs. They are also found to be at the leading edge of the market trends, implying their needs will be later experienced by following users.

Brand community is another important form of customer participation. It is "a specialized, non-geographically bound community, based on a structured set of social relations among admirers of a brand" (Muniz Jr and O'guinn, 2001). A core group of customers, who are deeply engaged with a brand and motivated by fun and identification, can actively participate in activities for the brand (Bagozzi and Dholakia, 2006; McAlexander et al., 2002). Füller et al. (2008) found creativity of the customer, identification with the community, and trust to the brand are important antecedents of customers' intention to share their knowledge on the brand for its improvement.

Crowd participation

Open innovation is on the same line with Lead User Theory, but it expands the sources of ideas from small parts of a customer group to a broader range of participants by redefining the boundary between a firm and its surrounding environment (Chesbrough and Crowther, 2006). The core concept of open innovation is associated with how a company uses ideas and knowledge of external players in its innovation process. A company that is more open to external channels and resources is more likely to generate a higher level of innovation (Laursen and Salter, 2006).

The scope of participation was extended to unspecific groups of crowds, which was led by new types of innovation, such as open source (Lakhani and Von Hippel, 2003) and crowdsourcing (Howe, 2008).

In open source setting, proposal and development of a project are operated by potentially many developers who are given access to the source materials. Developers who join open source software projects are found to have diverse sets of motivations including intrinsic (e.g., altruism, fun), internalized extrinsic (e.g., reputation, learning), and extrinsic (e.g., career, pay) (von Krogh et al., 2012).

Relatedly, crowdsourcing refers to a task that is proposed in the form of an open call to undefined crowds. Similar to open source projects, participants of crowdsourcing projects are motivated by several incentives such as learning opportunities, direct compensation, and appreciation by others (Leimeister et al., 2009).

Note

1 www.cannonfinancial.com/article/applied-behavioral-finance-an-introduction

References

Alpert, M. & Raiffa, H. 1982. A Progress Report on the Training of Probability Assessors. *In:* Kahneman, D., Slovic, P. & Tversky, A. (eds.) *Judgment Under Uncertainty: Heuristics and Biases.* Cambridge: Cambridge University Press.

Bagozzi, R. P. & Dholakia, U. M. 2006. Antecedents and Purchase Consequences of Customer Participation in Small Group Brand Communities. *International Journal of Research in Marketing*, 23, 45–61.

Barber, B. M. & Odean, T. 2001. Boys Will Be Boys: Gender, Overconfidence, and Common Stock Investment. *Quarterly Journal of Economics*, 116, 261–292.

Barclay, P. & Willer, R. 2007. Partner Choice Creates Competitive Altruism in Humans. *Proceedings of the Royal Society B: Biological Sciences*, 274, 749–753.

Bekkers, R. 2006. Traditional and Health-Related Philanthropy: The Role of Resources and Personality. *Social Psychology Quarterly*, 69, 349–366.

Bekkers, R. 2010. Who Gives What and When? A Scenario Study of Intentions to Give Time and Money. *Social Science Research*, 39, 369–381.

Bekkers, R. & Schuyt, T. 2008. And Who Is Your Neighbor? Explaining Denominational Differences in Charitable Giving and Volunteering in the Netherlands. *Review of Religious Research*, 50, 74–96.

Bennett, R. 2009. Impulsive Donation Decisions During Online Browsing of Charity Websites. *Journal of Consumer Behaviour*, 8, 116–134.

Berman, G. & Davidson, S. 2003. Do Donors Care? Some Australian Evidence. *Voluntas: International Journal of Voluntary and Nonprofit Organizations*, 14, 421–429.

Bottazzi, L., Da Rin, M. & Hellmann, T. (2016). The importance of trust for investment: Evidence from venture capital. *The Review of Financial Studies*, 29, 2283–2318.

Brown, J. R., Ivković, Z., Smith, P. A. & Weisbenner, S. 2008. Neighbors Matter: Causal Community Effects and Stock Market Participation. *The Journal of Finance*, 63, 1509–1531.

Bygrave, W. D. 1987. Syndicated Investments by Venture Capital Firms: A Networking Perspective. *Journal of Business Venturing*, 2, 139–154.

Chesbrough, H. & Crowther, A. K. 2006. Beyond High Tech: Early Adopters of Open Innovation in Other Industries. *R&D Management*, 36, 229–236.

Coleman, J. 1990. Norm-Generating Structures. *In:* Cook, K. S. & Levi, M. (eds.) *The Limits of Rationality*. Chicago: The University of Chicago Press.

Dawkins, R. 1976. *The Selfish Gene*. Oxford: Oxford University Press.

Filbeck, G., Hatfield, P. & Horvath, P. 2005. Risk Aversion and Personality Type. *The Journal of Behavioral Finance*, 6, 170–180.

Franke, N., Von Hippel, E. & Schreier, M. 2006. Finding Commercially Attractive User Innovations: A Test of Lead-User Theory*. *Journal of Product Innovation Management*, 23, 301–315.

Fried, V. H. & Hisrich, R. D. 1994. Toward a Model of Venture Capital Investment Decision Making. *Financial Management*, 23, 28–37.

Füller, J., Matzler, K. & Hoppe, M. 2008. Brand Community Members as a Source of Innovation. *Journal of Product Innovation Management*, 25, 608–619.

Gorman, M. & Sahlman, W. A. 1989. What Do Venture Capitalists Do? *Journal of Business Venturing*, 4, 231–248.

Grable, J. E. 2000. Financial Risk Tolerance and Additional Factors That Affect Risk Taking in Everyday Money Matters. *Journal of Business and Psychology*, 14, 625–630.

Grace, D. & Griffin, D. 2006. Exploring Conspicuousness in the Context of Donation Behaviour. *International Journal of Nonprofit and Voluntary Sector Marketing*, 11, 147–154.

Grace, D. & Griffin, D. 2009. Conspicuous Donation Behaviour: Scale Development and Validation. *Journal of Consumer Behaviour*, 8, 14–25.

Guy, B. S. & Patton, W. E. 1989. The Marketing of Altruistic Causes: Understanding Why People Help. *Journal of Consumer Marketing*, 6, 19–30.

Hall, J. & Hofer, C. W. 1993. Venture Capitalists' Decision Criteria in New Venture Evaluation. *Journal of Business Venturing*, 8, 25–42.

Hamilton, W. D. 1964. The Genetical Evolution of Social Behaviour. *Journal of Theoretical Biology*, 7, 1–16.

Handy, F. 2000. How We Beg: The Analysis of Direct Mail Appeals. *Nonprofit and Voluntary Sector Quarterly*, 29, 439–454.

Hawkes, K. 1991. Showing Off: Tests of an Hypothesis About Men's Foraging Goals. *Ethology and Sociobiology*, 12, 29–54.

Hisrich, R. D. & Jankowicz, A. D. 1990. Intuition in Venture Capital Decisions: An Exploratory Study Using a New Technique. *Journal of Business Venturing*, 5, 49–62.

Hong, H., Kubik, J. D. & Stein, J. C. 2004. Social Interaction and Stock-Market Participation. *The Journal of Finance*, 59, 137–163.

Howe, J. 2008. *Crowdsourcing: How the Power of the Crowd Is Driving the Future of Business*. New York: Random House.

Hsu, D. H. 2007. Experienced Entrepreneurial Founders, Organizational Capital, and Venture Capital Funding. *Research Policy*, 36, 722–741.

Jaffe, Y. & Yinon, Y. 1979. Retaliatory Aggression in Individuals and Groups. *European Journal of Social Psychology*, 9, 177–186.

Kahneman, D. & Tversky, A. 1979. Prospect Theory: An Analysis of Decision Under Risk. *Econometrica: Journal of the Econometric Society*, 47, 263–291.

Kottasz, R. 2004. How Should Charitable Organisations Motivate Young Professionals to Give Philanthropically? *International Journal of Nonprofit and Voluntary Sector Marketing*, 9, 9–27.

Lakhani, K. R. & Von Hippel, E. 2003. How Open Source Software Works. *Research Policy*, 32, 923–943.

Laursen, K. & Salter, A. 2006. Open for Innovation: The Role of Openness in Explaining Innovation Performance Among UK Manufacturing Firms. *Strategic Management Journal*, 27, 131–150.

Lea, M. & Spears, R. 1991. Computer-Mediated Communication, De-Individuation and Group Decision-Making. *International Journal of Man-Machine Studies*, 34, 283–301.

Le Bon, G. 1897. *The Crowd: A Study of the Popular Mind*. New York: Macmillan.

Lee, Y-K. & Chang, C-T. 2007. Who Gives What to Charity? Characteristics Affecting Donation Behavior. *Social Behavior and Personality: An International Journal*, 35, 1173–1180.

Leimeister, J. M., Huber, M., Bretschneider, U. & Krcmar, H. 2009. Leveraging Crowdsourcing: Activation-Supporting Components for It-Based Ideas Competition. *Journal of Management Information Systems*, 26, 197–224.

Leonard, R. J. 1995. From Parlor Games to Social Science: Von Neumann, Morgenstern, and the Creation of Game Theory 1928–1944. *Journal of Economic Literature*, 33, 730–761.

Lerner, J. 1994. The Syndication of Venture Capital Investments. *Financial Management*, 23, 16–27.

Lu Hsu, J., Liang, G-Y. & Tien, C-P. 2005. Social Concerns and Willingness to Support Charities. *Social Behavior & Personality: An International Journal*, 33.

Macmillan, I. C., Siegel, R. & Narasimha, P. N. S. 1985. Criteria Used by Venture Capitalists to Evaluate New Venture Proposals. *Journal of Business Venturing*, 1, 119–128.

Malmendier, U. & Nagel, S. 2011. Depression Babies: Do Macroeconomic Experiences Affect Risk Taking? *The Quarterly Journal of Economics*, 126, 373–416.
Markowitz, H. 1952. Portfolio Selection. *The Journal of Finance*, 7, 77–91.
Mcalexander, J. H., Schouten, J. W. & Koenig, H. F. 2002. Building Brand Community. *Journal of Marketing*, 66, 38–54.
Merchant, A. & Ford, J. 2008. Nostalgia and Giving to Charity: A Conceptual Framework for Discussion and Research. *International Journal of Nonprofit and Voluntary Sector Marketing*, 13, 13–30.
Micklewright, J. & Schnepf, S. V. 2009. Who Gives Charitable Donations for Overseas Development? *Journal of Social Policy*, 38, 317–341.
Montgomery, J. D. 1998. Toward a Role-Theoretic Conception of Embeddedness. *American Journal of Sociology*, 104, 92–125.
Muniz Jr, A. M. & O'Guinn, T. C. 2001. Brand Community. *Journal of Consumer Research*, 27, 412–432.
Nagy, R. A. & Obenberger, R. W. 1994. Factors Influencing Individual Investor Behavior. *Financial Analysts Journal*, 50, 63–68.
Noë, R. & Hammerstein, P. 1994. Biological Markets: Supply and Demand Determine the Effect of Partner Choice in Cooperation, Mutualism and Mating. *Behavioral Ecology and Sociobiology*, 35, 1–11.
Pessemier, E. A., Bemmaor, A. C. & Hanssens, D. M. 1977. Willingness to Supply Human Body Parts: Some Empirical Results. *Journal of Consumer Research*, 4, 131–140.
Radley, A. & Kennedy, M. 1995. Charitable Giving by Individuals: A Study of Attitudes and Practice. *Human Relations*, 48, 685–709.
Reicher, S. D. 1984. Social Influence in the Crowd: Attitudinal and Behavioural Effects of De-Individuation in Conditions of High and Low Group Salience*. *British Journal of Social Psychology*, 23, 341–350.
Reicher, S. D., Spears, R. & Postmes, T. 1995. A Social Identity Model of Deindividuation Phenomena. *European Review of Social Psychology*, 6, 161–198.
Riley Jr, W. B. & Chow, K. V. 1992. Asset Allocation and Individual Risk Aversion. *Financial Analysts Journal*, 48, 32–37.
Riquelme, H. & Rickards, T. 1992. Hybrid Conjoint Analysis: An Estimation Probe in New Venture Decisions. *Journal of Business Venturing*, 7, 505–518.
Sahlman, W. A. 1990. The Structure and Governance of Venture-Capital Organizations. *Journal of Financial Economics*, 27, 473–521.
Sargeant, A., Hudson, J. & West, D. C. 2008. Conceptualizing Brand Values in the Charity Sector: The Relationship Between Sector, Cause and Organization. *The Service Industries Journal*, 28, 615–632.
Scodel, A., Minas, J. S., Ratoosh, P. & Lipetz, M. 1959. Some Descriptive Aspects of Two-Person Non-Zero-Sum Games. *Journal of Conflict Resolution*, 114–119.
Sharpe, W. F. 1964. Capital Asset Prices: A Theory of Market Equilibrium Under Conditions of Risk. *The Journal of Finance*, 19, 425–442.
Shefrin, H. M. & Statman, M. 1984. Explaining Investor Preference for Cash Dividends. *Journal of Financial Economics*, 13, 253–282.
Sherry Jr, J. F. 1983. Gift Giving in Anthropological Perspective. *Journal of Consumer Research*, 10, 157–168.
Shier, M. L. & Handy, F. 2012. Understanding Online Donor Behavior: The Role of Donor Characteristics, Perceptions of the Internet, Website and Program, and

Influence from Social Networks. *International Journal of Nonprofit and Voluntary Sector Marketing*, 17, 219–230.

Sojka, J. 1986. Understanding Donor Behaviour: A Classification Paradigm. *Advances in Consumer Research*, 13, 240–245.

Sunden, A. E. & Surette, B. J. 1998. Gender Differences in the Allocation of Assets in Retirement Savings Plans. *The American Economic Review*, 88, 207–211.

Thaler, R. H. & Shefrin, H. M. 1981. An Economic Theory of Self-Control. *The Journal of Political Economy*, 89, 392–406.

Trivers, R. L. 1971. The Evolution of Reciprocal Altruism. *Quarterly Review of Biology*, 35–57.

Turner, R. H. & Killian, L. M. 1957. *Collective Behavior*. Oxford: Prentice-Hall.

Tversky, A. & Kahneman, D. (1974). Judgment Under Uncertainty: Heuristics and Biases. *Science*, 185(4157), 1124–1131.

Ueda, M. 2004. Banks Versus Venture Capital: Project Evaluation, Screening, and Expropriation. *The Journal of Finance*, 59, 601–621.

Urban, G. L. & Von Hippel, E. 1988. Lead User Analyses for the Development of New Industrial Products. *Management Science*, 34, 569–582.

Von Hippel, E. 1986. Lead Users: A Source of Novel Product Concepts. *Management Science*, 32, 791–805.

Von Hippel, E. & Katz, R. 2002. Shifting Innovation to Users via Toolkits. *Management Science*, 48, 821–833.

Von Krogh, G., Haefliger, S., Spaeth, S. & Wallin, M. W. 2012. Carrots and Rainbows: Motivation and Social Practice in Open Source Software Development. *MIS Quarterly*, 36, 649–676.

Wang, H. & Hanna, S. 1997. Does Risk Tolerance Decrease with Age. *Financial Counseling and Planning*, 8, 27–31.

West, P. 2004. *Conspicuous Compassion: Why Sometimes It Really Is Cruel to Be Kind*. London: Civitas.

Wynne-Edwards, V. C. 1962. *Animal Dispersion in Relation to Social Behaviour*. New York: Hafner Pub. Co.

Zider, B. 1998. How Venture Capital Works. *Harvard Business Review*, 76, 131–139.

Zimbardo, P. G. 1969. *The Human Choice: Individuation, Reason, and Order Versus Deindividuation, Impulse, and Chaos*. Nebraska Symposium on Motivation, Lincoln: University of Nebraska Press.

4 What we know (and don't know) about crowdfunding

In this chapter, we review the literature on crowdfunding, focusing on important factors influencing individual contributors' funding decision and thus what drives successful crowdfunding campaigns.

Influential factors affecting crowdfunding success and contributor decision-making

First, creators play a significant role in determining a campaign's success. For example, creators' social information and educational backgrounds are closely associated to the success of a campaign (Mollick, 2014). Boeuf et al. (2014) found disclosure of personal information about creators has positive influences on crowdfunding success because it helps them obtain higher levels of trust from potential contributors. Frydrych et al. (2014) also argue that information on the creator adds legitimacy to the campaign, attracting more contributors as a result. Creators' social networks also act as key factors influencing crowdfunding success. Zheng et al. (2014) showed how creators' social network ties and experience in funding other campaigns affect crowdfunding success. Importantly, the internal social capital of creators developed inside a crowdfunding platform contributes significantly toward success of a crowdfunding campaign (Colombo et al., 2015). Antonenko et al. (2014) suggested that intensive communication efforts of creators, such as reacting promptly to questions and providing frequent status updates, are positively associated with crowdfunding success. Crowdfunding success is also promoted when contributors perceive the creator as passionate (Davis et al., 2017).

Second, information and disclosure of campaign quality and characteristics are important to crowdfunding success. One of my research, with Young-Gul Kim, found that reward value and societal contribution of a campaign are critical characteristics affecting crowdfunding success (Ryu and Kim, 2018). Explicit information on project quality, such as awards received, serves as effective cues for potential contributors (Ciuchta et al., 2016). Linguistic styles in campaign descriptions also affect the success of crowdfunding campaigns (Parhankangas and Renko, 2017; Allison et al., 2017). Linguistic styles that make a campaign more understandable and relatable to potential contributors support the success of crowdfunding campaigns, especially in the context of societal campaigns (Parhankangas and Renko, 2017). Relatedly, Allison et al. (2017) found a cognitive message that is logically persuasive and affective cues that are is emotionally persuasive influence crowdfunding campaign success. Davis et al. (2017) found that contributors' decisions to pledge are positively influenced by perceived product creativity.

Third, campaign design and information on campaign progress are other influential factors. Some design components, such as campaign duration, goal amount, and inclusion of a video on a campaign page, are all associated with success (Mollick, 2014). For example, Mollick (2014) suggests that potential contributors are more likely to fund campaigns with realistic funding goals and durations. Campaign progress posted on the campaign page suggest much information. Most of all, contributor participation in the early stages is essential for signaling campaign quality and subsequently attracting more contributors with a snowball effect (Agrawal et al., 2015; Burtch et al., 2013; Colombo et al., 2015). Colombo et al. (2015) showed that success of a campaign is fully mediated by the funding amount that contributors collected in the campaign's early days. More specifically, Kim and Viswanathan (2018) argued that information about early contributors with expertise in the domain of the campaigns has a distinct influence on later contributors. Relatedly, Kuppuswamy and Bayus (2017) showed the importance of goal proximity in explaining fund timing. Specifically, they found that people are more likely to contribute when a campaign approaches its funding goal, when they can make an impact on the ultimate success of fundraising, than after the funding goal has been reached. In the same vein, Dai and Zhang (2019) found that campaigns tend to collect funding faster right before meeting their funding goals compared to right after. It suggests that contributors are willing to contribute to the campaign's success in obtaining the preset goal amount. Interestingly, the effect is intensified in the case of the campaigns with prosocial objectives and those launched by a single person.

Then, who are more likely (and earlier) to join a crowdfunding campaign? Research shows that crowdfunders who are experts (Kim and Viswanathan, 2018) or local (Kang et al., 2017; Agrawal et al., 2015; Giudici et al., 2018) tend to participate in crowdfunding earlier. Local contributors are more likely to pledge at the early stages of the funding period than distant contributors, and they are less sensitive to peer effects. They are also less sensitive to information about the cumulative amount of funding (Lin and Viswanathan, 2015). Contributors are also more likely to contribute to "culturally similar" creators' campaign (Burtch et al., 2014). From the perspective of platform design, permission to control the disclosure of funding information has been found to increase the number of contributions and simultaneously to decrease the amount of each contribution (Burtch et al., 2015).

Implications from the current crowdfunding literature

The current body of literature on crowdfunding provides some implications.

The literature supports the view that crowdfunding possesses both common aspects as a funding channel and distinguished aspects as a new type of channel.

Crowdfunding is similar to traditional funding sources such as VCs in that potential contributors make decisions to contribute based on a set of information they collect through the crowdfunding platform. For example, evaluation of creators is important in the crowdfunding context, which is similar to what traditional investors do with founders. The differences are that they may leverage different types of information from that of traditional players. Campaign progress is a more critical factor in the context of crowdfunding.

For potential creators, the literature provides some guidelines. Most of all, different-quality information and effective communication of that information are critical for any type of crowdfunding campaign. A strand of research identified specific attributes or characteristics of campaigns and their creators that boost individual contributors' behavior and thus crowdfunding success. Those results can provide practical aid in this regard.

More importantly, in addition to polishing the campaign itself, understanding social aspects of crowdfunding is critical to reach the goal amount. Creators must understand the importance of earlier pledges and momentum throughout the campaign progress from the earlier performance. They are expected to develop a strategy to collect a group of early contributors according to the nature of the campaign. Strong social capital of a creator from inside and outside of the crowdfunding platform should help the creator initiate this momentum for crowdfunding success.

Although, previous literature found some implicative mechanisms of crowdfunding, the current body of literature has several limitations that indicate future research directions. Most of all, whereas the literature validated the influencers of campaign success and individual contributors' behaviors, a leading, detailed theoretical mechanism of exactly how a specific influencer affects campaign performance and contributor behavior has not been found. Future research can find more theoretical evidence for the findings so far based on theorizing the underlying mechanism in the specific context of crowdfunding.

Moreover, the main research streams on crowdfunding have focused on explicit factors related to creators and their projects affecting the success of a crowdfunding project, but less attention has been paid to motivation of players on both sides. Creators and contributors join crowdfunding with different motivations (Gerber et al., 2012; Ryu and Kim, 2016; Ryu and Kim, 2018). A few pioneering studies dealt with motivations in the crowdfunding context, but the literature has not established how those motivations interact with other factors, such as campaign characteristics. To fill this gap, future research can delve deeply into how different motivations interrelate with crowdfunding success and contributor behaviors. Specifically, because motivations are psychological factors, examining how motivations interact with other attributes such as demographic, campaign, or platform characteristics could be important considerations.

Finally, the extant literature on crowdfunding has focused on the success of campaigns "inside" crowdfunding platforms. Recently, the perspective is expanding to post-campaign phenomena by examining the effects of crowdfunding success on follow-up performance of ventures (Roma et al., 2017; Ryu et al., 2018), which will be further discussed in Chapter 11. Nevertheless, we still don't know much about how crowdfunding can influence entrepreneurial organizations' long-term performance and thus survival. Regarding this gap between the findings from previous literature, and the expected role of crowdfunding in longer terms, future research can identify how crowdfunding affects subsequent performance in different aspects.

References

Agrawal, A., Catalini, C. & Goldfarb, A. 2015. Crowdfunding: Geography, Social Networks, and the Timing of Investment Decisions. *Journal of Economics & Management Strategy*, 24, 253–274.

Allison, T. H., Davis, B. C., Webb, J. W. & Short, J. C. 2017. Persuasion in Crowdfunding: An Elaboration Likelihood Model of Crowdfunding Performance. *Journal of Business Venturing*, 32, 707–725.

Antonenko, P. D., Lee, B. R. & Kleinheksel, A. 2014. Trends in the Crowdfunding of Educational Technology Startups. *TechTrends*, 58, 36–41.

Boeuf, B., Darveau, J. & Legoux, R. 2014. Financing Creativity: Crowdfunding as a New Approach for Theatre Projects. *International Journal of Arts Management*, 16, 33–48.

Burtch, G., Ghose, A. & Wattal, S. 2013. An Empirical Examination of the Antecedents and Consequences of Contribution Patterns in Crowd-Funded Markets. *Information Systems Research*, 24, 499–519.

Burtch, G., Ghose, A. & Wattal, S. 2014. Cultural Differences and Geography as Determinants of Online Prosocial Lending. *MIS Quarterly*, 38, 773–794.

Burtch, G., Ghose, A. & Wattal, S. 2015. The Hidden Cost of Accommodating Crowdfunder Privacy Preferences: A Randomized Field Experiment. *Management Science*, 61, 949–962.

Ciuchta, M. P., Letwin, C., Stevenson, R. M. & Mcmahon, S. R. 2016. Regulatory Focus and Information Cues in a Crowdfunding Context. *Journal of Applied Psychology*, 65, 490–514.

Colombo, M. G., Franzoni, C. & Rossi-Lamastra, C. 2015. Internal Social Capital and the Attraction of Early Contributions in Crowdfunding. *Entrepreneurship Theory and Practice*, 39, 75–100.

Dai, H. & Zhang, D. J. 2019. Prosocial Goal Pursuit in Crowdfunding: Evidence from Kickstarter. *Journal of Marketing Research*, 56, 498–517.

Davis, B. C., Hmieleski, K. M., Webb, J. W. & Coombs, J. E. 2017. Funders' Positive Affective Reactions to Entrepreneurs' Crowdfunding Pitches: The Influence of Perceived Product Creativity and Entrepreneurial Passion. *Journal of Business Venturing*, 32, 90–106.

Frydrych, D., Bock, A. J., Kinder, T. & Koeck, B. 2014. Exploring Entrepreneurial Legitimacy in Reward-Based Crowdfunding. *Venture Capital*, 16, 247–269.

Gerber, E. M., Hui, J. S. & Kuo, P. 2012. Crowdfunding: Why People Are Motivated to Post and Fund Projects on Crowdfunding Platforms. *Proceedings of the International Workshop on Design, Influence, and Social Technologies: Techniques, Impacts and Ethics*, Northwestern University, Evanston, IL. Retrieved on March.

Giudici, G., Guerini, M. & Rossi-Lamastra, C. 2018. Reward-Based Crowdfunding of Entrepreneurial Projects: The Effect of Local Altruism and Localized Social Capital on Proponents' Success. *Small Business Economics*, 50, 307–324.

Kang, L., Jiang, Q. & Tan, C-H. 2017. Remarkable Advocates: An Investigation of Geographic Distance and Social Capital for Crowdfunding. *Information & Management*, 54, 336–348.

Kim, K. & Viswanathan, S. 2018. The 'Experts' in the Crowd: The Role of Experienced Investors in a Crowdfunding Market. *MIS Quarterly*, Forthcoming.

Kuppuswamy, V. & Bayus, B. L. 2017. Does My Contribution to Your Crowdfunding Project Matter? *Journal of Business Venturing*, 32, 72–89.

Lin, M. & Viswanathan, S. 2015. Home Bias in Online Investments: An Empirical Study of an Online Crowdfunding Market. *Management Science*, 62, 1393–1414.

Mollick, E. 2014. The Dynamics of Crowdfunding: An Exploratory Study. *Journal of Business Venturing*, 29, 1–16.

Parhankangas, A. & Renko, M. 2017. Linguistic Style and Crowdfunding Success Among Social and Commercial Entrepreneurs. *Journal of Business Venturing*, 32, 215–236.

Roma, P., Petruzzelli, A. M. & Perrone, G. 2017. From the Crowd to the Market: The Role of Reward-Based Crowdfunding Performance in Attracting Professional Investors. *Research Policy*, 49, 1606–1628.

Ryu, S., Kim, K. & Hahn, J. 2018. The Effect of Crowdfunding Success on Subsequent Financing Outcomes of Start-Ups. *Social Science Research Network*. Available at: https://ssrn.com/abstract=2938285.

Ryu, S. & Kim, Y-G. 2016. A Typology of Crowdfunding Sponsors: Birds of a Feather Flock Together? *Electronic Commerce Research and Applications*, 16, 43–54.

Ryu, S. & Kim, Y-G. 2018. Money Is Not Everything: A Typology of Crowdfunding Project Creators. *Journal of Strategic Information Systems*, 27, 350–368.

Zheng, H., Li, D., Wu, J. & Xu, Y. 2014. The Role of Multidimensional Social Capital in Crowdfunding: A Comparative Study in China and US. *Information & Management*, 51, 488–496.

Part 2
Beauty of crowdfunding

5 Creativity

Sundance Film Festival and Kickstarter

Matthew Lessner, an independent movie director, headed to the Sundance Film Festival with his movie *The Woods* in 2011. With more than 50,000 attendees in recent years, taking place annually in Park City, Utah, the Sundance Film Festival is one of the largest and most prestigious independent film festivals in the United States.[1] Although his story concluded with a happy ending, its beginning was discouraging. He financed his project initially with credit cards for the first month of shooting, but as the economic conditions worsened, his work could not be developed for more than a year and thus remained as an incomplete piece. Later, a friend introduced a new idea to reinitiate production. It was Kickstarter. He was not a tech-savvy person but tried his best to prepare the pitch for a crowdfunding campaign, and the result was more than what he expected. He raised $11,584 from 95 contributors to finish the film and make history as the first movie campaign in Kickstarter to make it to the Sundance Film Festival.

Beginning with Matthew Lessner's campaign, from 2011 to 2018, 115 crowdfunded films in Kickstarter have premiered at the Sundance Film Festival.[2] For example, of the Festival's 200 films (among around 9,000 submissions every year) in 2012, 17 films were crowdfunded via Kickstarter.[3] A statistic indicated approximately 10% of films submitted are accepted into the prestigious independent film festivals. The Sundance Film Festival, the South by Southwest Festival (SXSW), and the Tribeca Film Festival all have benefited from Kickstarter.[4,5]

Sundance Institute, the nonprofit organization behind the festival, has been strategically collaborating with Kickstarter to support young and promising filmmakers who do not possess the same reputation that the festival itself has. With the funds from Kickstarter campaigns, filmmakers can move forward boldly with their projects and bring their creativity to life. While they may own the rights and retain all revenue from their films, the funds can be expended for different purposes, such as post production, theatrical booking, publicity, and advertising. This approach is noble in several aspects. First, the filmmakers can overcome financial restrictions when they might find it difficult to manage fundraisers by themselves. Second, they are not necessarily required to hand over the screening rights of their films to major distributors. Third, they can build awareness and outreach to potential audiences in advance of releasing the films.

In addition to films, many other creative products and services have been supported using the crowdfunding platform. Technology and design-related campaigns are among the most dominant categories in reward-based crowdfunding platforms, but different categories, such as music, comics, dance, and theater, also benefit from the introduction of crowdfunding.

For example, many innovative hardware products were invented through crowdfunding, including a first generation of smartwatches and VR headsets. Pebble, a first generation of smartwatches, connected to iOS and Android devices to display notifications and messages on its screen, was able to raise more than $10 million from almost 69,000 backers on Kickstarter, hitting its $100,000 goal on the first day of the campaign.

Eric Migicovsky, the founder of Pebble Technology Corporation that developed Pebble, had raised seed funding from angel investors but was unable to raise additional funds. Due to the inability to raise further funds, he turned to crowdfunding in April 2012. In May 2012, the campaign closed successfully, and at the time it held the world record for the most funding raised in a crowdfunding campaign. In 2015, the company launched its second generation of smartwatches, and they were similarly funded through Kickstarter, raising $20.3 million from more than 75,000 backers, breaking records for the site again.[6]

Oculus Rift, another crowdfunding blockbuster, was also funded with a Kickstarter campaign launched in August 2012, right after Pebble's sensational success. It was just after Oculus VR, the company behind Oculus Rift, was founded as an independent company in July 2012, following the demonstration of the Oculus Rift prototype in June 2012.[7] The campaign proved successful, raising $2.4 million, far surpassing the $250,000 goal.[8] After some rounds of following investments, in March 2014, Facebook purchased Oculus VR for $2 billion.[9]

Without crowdfunding, those brilliant and creative products may not have become part of our lives.

Fueling creativity

The first advantage of crowdfunding is creativity. Crowdfunding supports creative work in diverse sectors. Countless creative works, from fine arts to design and technology, have been introduced to the world via crowdfunding platforms. Creators share their creative ideas on crowdfunding platforms in anticipation of financial and nonfinancial support from potential contributors. A series of indie movies, a smartwatch, a multifunctional jacket, and so on and on – each of these creative ideas might have met their last flicker in a picture drawn in a creator's head or on paper without crowdfunding.

Not surprisingly, crowdfunding platforms, which perform as mediators between creators and contributors, frequently advocate creativity as a core value to be promoted. This value is particularly presented through their mission statements, which refer to the aspiration to support creativity. For example, Kickstarter's mission is to "bring creative projects to life."[10] Similarly, Indiegogo's mission is to "empower people to unite around ideas that matter to them and together make those ideas come to life."[11] Other crowdfunding platforms are also positioning themselves in comparable positions. Such norms of appreciating creativity may promote the likelihood that a creative campaign is introduced on a crowdfunding platform and the campaign generates positive reactions from potential contributors.

Creativity, by definition, is the development of products or processes that are both novel and useful (Hennessey and Amabile, 2010). Product or process is evaluated to be novel if nobody has been aware of it before; it is considered to be useful when it provides some value for community or society. On one hand, in the crowdfunding context, a campaign with only novel ideas, but no usefulness, may draw attention from a few "geeks" but would not obtain considerable funding from the crowd. On the other hand, if another campaign possesses only certain value, but is not new or innovative, potential contributors may have no interest in the campaign at all. Considering the systems how crowdfunding is processed, crowdfunding itself can perform as a filter to pinpoint more creative work. Thus, campaigns that are more creative will be in closer alignment with the objective of crowdfunding, and with the expectations of potential contributors, and will be more successful at raising funds.

In this regard, crowdfunding encourages and promotes creativity in a most inventive way. Supporting a crowdfunding campaign collaboratively is an approach to mingle ideas and produce new ones, fueling creativity. Both creators and contributors can influence the progress, and thus outcome of the campaign, by interacting with each other and developing the idea online. Crowdfunding platforms are especially useful for young and early-career creators who are building their identity as the platforms provide an opportunity for their creativity to be recognized and appreciated by potential contributors. It definitely has advantages for more established creators because they can leverage their stable supporter base in initiating momentum and spreading the word to wider networks. Altogether, crowdfunding is an efficacious way to initiate relationships beginning with a relatively small contribution and returning a reward (or other benefits) that can expand to cultivate both the creative and financial resilience of diverse creative sectors.

What researchers have found so far

Considering the role of crowdfunding in encouraging creativity across domains, a stream of research has tackled how crowdfunding supports creativity.

How crowdfunding supports creativity

Crowdfunding promotes different types of individuals and groups to pitch their creative ideas to potential contributors in expectation of financial support. In addition to this main benefit of crowdfunding, creators and contributors also leverage the platforms to expose creative thoughts, explore creative inspiration, and initiate new connections with other creative entities. As a dedicated supporting tool for creativity, crowdfunding encourages people to get their creative ideas shared, identified, endorsed, and supported (Kuo and Gerber, 2012).

According to a preliminary study of Kuo and Gerber (2012), crowdfunding can encourage creativity throughout the four different phases: collect, relate, create, and donate. First, at the collect phase, people may search previous work for building up new creative ideas and projects. As most crowdfunding platforms collect, store, and provide information of all past and current projects, potential creators and contributors are able to search and review key concepts and representations of creativity from successful projects (in most cases) and unsuccessful projects (in few cases). Second, at the relate phase, creators can validate their creative ideas or projects, and contributors can offer feedback on the creators' projects. Throughout most creative processes, collaboration with other individuals and advice from experts are the most important parts. Crowdfunding platforms help these activities become accessible and effortless. Creators publicly collect comments and evaluation from their contributors as they launch projects in crowdfunding platforms. Platform operators provide online community-like features for promoting these validation and feedback activities, which are essential for every stage of the creative work. Third, at the create phase, crowdfunding helps people associate themselves with the generation of creative ideas. Both creators and contributors can create their own associations of campaigns in platforms. It also offers space for examination of new ideas, specifically for creators. Creators can learn by doing. Crowdfunding allows them to experiment and try out their creativity as they launch a project by lowering entry barriers and risk. Finally, at the donate phase, crowdfunding platforms publicize processes and results of all campaigns to connect them to the community. Crowdfunding platforms are linked to different types of media, including press media (e.g., newspapers, broadcasting) and social media, to distribute creative work from crowdfunding campaigns. Creators leverage social media to encourage people to join their campaigns. Contributors view articles from press media and receive messages from their social media connections to follow creative work. Those activities help promote traffic to the crowdfunding platforms.

Crowdfunding also supports the creative process by promoting collaboration between creators and their contributors (Zheng et al., 2018). In the crowdfunding context, contributors can produce more value in the production and marketing processes of products and services compared to traditional business settings. The engagement of contributors in a crowdfunding campaign can be called a cocreation process. Contributors may involve themselves in the whole process of crowdfunding, from product design to development and production, in addition to financially supporting the campaign. Contributors' cocreation activity includes sharing ideas with the creators about early prototypes and responding to the campaigns' updates and other contributors' comments. They add more creativity to the campaigns. Cocreation with contributors provides remarkable value to creative aspects of crowdfunding as it is especially helpful for creative idea generation and innovation. Cocreation activities also generate positive consequences on the contributor side. Contributors may perceive the campaigns they cocreate to be more creative, thus adding more value to them in addition to the initial value from the product itself. More importantly, cocreation activities contribute to enhancing the associations between campaigns and their contributors by potentially building emotional attachment. Although contributors do not retain actual ownership of the outcome of campaigns in reward-based crowdfunding, they may experience certain levels of psychological ownership, a feeling of possession that allows contributors to consider the campaign as an extension of the self. With psychological ownership, the level of contributor commitment and contributions to the campaigns substantially escalate. When a contributor actively commits to the campaign implementation, he/she devotes more time and resources to the campaign. He/she has more communication with the creator and other contributors during the processes. Moreover, he/she may contribute to the campaign by preaching it to social networks, which could be potential contributors, during and/or after the campaign. In conclusion, crowdfunding is a remarkable supporting platform and tool for creativity throughout the whole process of creative works.

How creativity of crowdfunding campaigns is related to crowdfunding performance

As creativity is a key component of any crowdfunding campaign, potential contributors extensively evaluate how much creative a focal crowdfunding campaign is when they make a decision to support the campaign. A strand of studies examined and found the implicative association between creativity of crowdfunding campaigns and performance.

Overall, perceived creativity of crowdfunding products, which are expected outputs of the crowdfunding campaigns, is positively related to campaign performance (Davis et al., 2017). Potential contributors may judge whether a product is novel and useful relative to its existing associates. They may evaluate the product's level of creativity as an indicator of potential performance and the creator's capability for managing and progressing the campaign. If they evaluate a crowdfunding product as purposeful and value generating, they may participate in supporting the crowdfunding campaign. Moreover, regarding the tendency that individuals experience positive emotion through observing and committing to creative work and creative products and campaigns, this potentially promotes affective reactions among contributors, catalyzing their participation.

The association between creativity and crowdfunding performance counts on campaign characteristics (Calic and Mosakowski, 2016). For example, creators with a sustainability orientation, focusing on either social or environmental value, will be more likely to generate creative products and, consequently, achieve higher performance compared to others with completely commercial campaigns. This is because a sustainability orientation drives creators to confront the tensions between economic values and social/environmental considerations, and it should lead to more creativity for discovering more innovative and meaningful solutions. Relatedly, dimensions of innovativeness in crowdfunding campaigns affects campaign outcome, namely, incremental versus radical innovativeness (Chan and Parhankangas, 2017). Incremental innovativeness refers to a character of novelty that is less dramatic and produces accumulative improvement of existing resources or capabilities, whereas radical innovativeness reflects a character of novelty that is more dramatic and unique and may generate paradigm-shifting resources or capabilities. Crowdfunding campaigns with greater incremental innovativeness, which are more understandable and generate more value for overall contributors, may result in more positive campaign outcomes. By comparison, campaigns that feature greater radical innovativeness, which are riskier to develop, and more difficult for contributors to comprehend, result in less positive campaign outcomes. Contributors who are motivated to help creators bring creative ideas to life may be less willing to support radically innovative campaigns because they are more likely to perceive the potential benefits of radically innovative campaigns as uncertain and risky to acquire, considerably lowering their willingness to support. These campaigns and their potential outputs are mostly less comprehensible, risky to develop, and hard to suggest feedback for, which diminishes potential cocreation activities during the crowdfunding process. More importantly, most contributors often lack the special knowledge required to understand the technologies behind the campaigns and thus may be uncertain about the benefits from the campaign results. One potential solution for filling in the gap between radically innovative campaigns and potential contributors and mitigating the negative effect of radical innovativeness on campaign performance is to leverage components of incremental innovativeness in a campaign. If creators, who are launching radically innovative campaigns, could find a part of incremental innovativeness in their campaigns and address the part to potential contributors in an uncomplicated manner, the approach may help them comprehend and appreciate the aspects of radical innovativeness more. For example, if creators suggest how the results from radical innovativeness improve the current status of daily life and practice, contributors could readily recognize the potential value of the campaigns.

How the crowds perceive creativity differently from experts

Related to the different responses to radical and incremental innovativeness, contributors in the crowdfunding context may differ from ordinary experts in evaluating creativity and thus expected quality of crowdfunding campaigns. For tackling the issue, Mollick and Nanda (2015) studied theater campaigns in Kickstarter, examining how evaluation of the crowds on certain projects differs from the expert evaluation and how the difference implies the role of crowdfunding in promoting creativity. They recruited expert evaluators who specialize in judging theater-related applications for funding institutions and asked them to evaluate randomly selected theater campaigns in Kickstarter, including both successful and unsuccessful ones.

Overall, they found remarkable compromise between the crowds and the experts in funding decisions. Campaigns that were successfully funded by the contributors on Kickstarter obtained consistently higher evaluation from experts. The results suggest crowds are generally similar to experts in their evaluation on creativity and decisions on which campaigns to support. When contributors and experts contradict, it is much more likely to be a case in which the contributors supported campaigns that experts would not. There was a clear pattern in terms of the characteristics of campaigns that are favored by the crowds over experts, including multiple tiers of reward plans and extra updates. This suggests the crowds may place emphasis on campaign design aspects in addition to creativity itself, which is different from the emphasis of expert evaluation on creativity. Examining the longer-term outcomes of the campaigns, more importantly, they found no differences in quantitative or qualitative aspects between campaigns funded by crowdfunding alone and those that were chosen by both the contributors and experts. They are equally likely to continue to perform, and many of these performances enjoyed commercial success, higher ticket sales, and positive critical recognition. The results are implicative because it suggests crowds do not underperform in comparison to experts in evaluating creativity and thus potential performance of campaigns.

For sustainable creativity

The basic crowdfunding model, collecting small amounts of funding from crowds to support a specific campaign, has evolved into diverse derivational models to promote creativity in different domains. Among those, the subscription-based crowdfunding model, allowing creators to solicit money from their audiences on a monthly basis, or per work basis, and distribute their work directly to them, has been recently drawing remarkable attention from both creator and contributor sides. Even though it has never been more accessible for creators to create, and distribute their contents through online platforms such as YouTube and Instagram, it is still challenging even for the creators with large and loyal audiences to monetize the audience bases. Moreover, they are struggling to figure out who pays attention to their work and why, which is essential information for them to develop their creative work. The subscription-based crowdfunding model can tackle those issues in effective ways.

In earlier 2013, Jack Conte was disheartened by the challenge that he confronted as a musician supporting himself as a creator in the digital age.[12] Conte spent $10,000 of his own money for producing an original sci-fi–themed music video. He posted the video on YouTube, and it was a hit; soon accomplished a million views. But Conte's share of revenue from advertisements with the views was about $150. He thought it was so weird to see such a disparity between the value that he contributed to the society and the value that the society returned to him. The predicament was almost universal for every type of creator. He suddenly came up with a solution: what if fans pay a few dollars per month to creators so that they can keep being engaged with their creative work? This idea is developed into Patreon, a subscription-based crowdfunding platform. Whereas reward-based crowdfunding, such as Kickstarter and Indiegogo, focus on specific projects, Patreon asks fans to support creators a subscription basis. This design allows different types of creators, from fine artists to video bloggers, to turn these individual sponsorships into a substantial and continuous income base.

Launched in May 2013, Patreon immediately hit the market and has been growing rapidly.[13] As of January 2019, it obtained 3 million contributors (patrons at Patreon) who are active sponsors to 100,000 monthly active creators. The creators earned $300 million in 2018 alone via the Patreon platform.[14] Creators doubled their income compared to where they were before joining the platform. Although creators themselves could set different tiers of patronage, from $1 to more than $100, average patronage per contributor is around $12. Creators can gain upward of 90% of the total patronage, with 5% of fees going to the platform, Patreon, and the rest to payment-related costs. Creators earn from a couple hundred dollars to tens of thousands each month.[15]

In 2012, musician Amanda Palmer set a new record by raising more than $1.2 million on Kickstarter to fund her new album.[16] From her perspective, the core value of the Kickstarter campaign was that it allowed her to create art and proved that the community supports her potential. But, she hasn't returned to the platform, even though she highly appreciates its value. Rather she turned into Patreon because she thought the original reward-based model, specifically campaign based, is not sustainable for musicians like her as those types of creators desire to make serial content in relatively short cycles. They are more likely to ask people to subscribe monthly. In Patreon, patrons pledge to pay a fixed amount per work. Their support is changing creators' worlds, including Amanda's: as of 2019, more than 15,000 patrons have supported her 76 creations, and it is still continuing.[17]

Key takeaways

- Crowdfunding encourages, supports, and fuels creative work in diverse sectors. Creators share their creative ideas on crowdfunding platforms, such as Kickstarter and Indiegogo, in anticipation of financial and nonfinancial supports from contributors.
- In addition to the financial benefit of crowdfunding, creators and contributors also leverage the platforms to expose creative thoughts, explore creative inspiration, and initiate new connections to other creative entities.
- Creativity of crowdfunding campaigns and products is positively related to campaign performance. Contributors may evaluate the level of creativity as an indicator of potential performance and the creator's capability for progressing the campaign.
- Literature found remarkable agreement in evaluation of creativity and funding decisions between crowds and experts. Campaigns that were successfully crowdfunded obtained consistently higher evaluation from experts. When crowds and experts contradict, it is much more likely to be a case where the crowds supported campaigns that experts would not.

- Subscription-based crowdfunding, such as Patreon, allows creators to solicit money from their audiences on a monthly basis, or per work basis, and distribute their work directly. The model tackles the issue of sustainability in the creative sector.

Notes

1. www.sundance.org/festivals/sundance-film-festival
2. www.theverge.com/2017/5/1/15506936/sundance-institute-kickstarter-columbus-unrest-distribution
3. https://creators.vice.com/en_au/article/wnzy5b/kickstarter-films-dominate-sundance-this-year
4. https://mediadecoder.blogs.nytimes.com/2012/01/30/at-sundance-kickstarter-resembled-a-movie-studio-but-without-the-egos/
5. www.wired.com/2012/03/getting-to-sxsw-kickstarter/
6. In 2016, Pebble closed their subsequent Time 2 series watches and refunded Kickstarter contributors due to financial issues. In December 2016, Pebble announced that the company would be closed and would no longer produce or support any devices. Pebble's intellectual property was acquired by Fitbit, a wearable technology company.
7. Palmer Luckey, a founder of Oculus VR, started Oculus Rift as a side project from his parents' garage.
8. www.kickstarter.com/projects/1523379957/oculus-rift-step-into-the-game
9. https://techcrunch.com/2014/07/21/facebooks-acquisition-of-oculus-closes-now-official
10. www.kickstarter.com/about
11. www.indiegogo.com/about/our-story
12. www.fastcompany.com/40457448/how-crowdfunding-site-patreon-is-helping-artists-build-media-empires
13. www.fastcompany.com/90295558/patreon-is-on-track-to-reach-1-billion-in-total-payments-to-creators
14. www.patreon.com/about
15. https://graphtreon.com/top-patreon-creators
16. https://blog.patreon.com/amanda-palmer-is-home
17. www.patreon.com/amandapalmer/overview

References

Calic, G. & Mosakowski, E. 2016. Kicking Off Social Entrepreneurship: How A Sustainability Orientation Influences Crowdfunding Success. *Journal of Management Studies*, 53, 738–767.

Chan, C. S. R. & Parhankangas, A. 2017. Crowdfunding Innovative Ideas: How Incremental and Radical Innovativeness Influence Funding Outcomes. *Entrepreneurship Theory and Practice*, 41, 237–263.

Davis, B. C., Hmieleski, K. M., Webb, J. W. & Coombs, J. E. 2017. Funders' Positive Affective Reactions to Entrepreneurs' Crowdfunding Pitches: The Influence of Perceived Product Creativity and Entrepreneurial Passion. *Journal of Business Venturing*, 32, 90–106.

Hennessey, B. A. & Amabile, T. M. 2010. Creativity. *Annual Review of Psychology*, 61, 569–598.

Kuo, P-Y. & Gerber, E. 2012. *Design Principles: Crowdfunding as a Creativity Support Tool. CHI'12 Extended Abstracts on Human Factors in Computing Systems.* New York: ACM, 1601–1606.

Mollick, E. R. & Nanda, R. 2015. Wisdom or Madness? Comparing Crowds with Expert Evaluation in Funding the Arts. *Management Science*, 62, 1533–1553.

Zheng, H., Xu, B., Zhang, M. & Wang, T. 2018. Sponsor's Cocreation and Psychological Ownership in Reward-Based Crowdfunding. *Information Systems Journal*, 28, 1213–1238.

6 Diversity

Between flower-decorated canes and potato salad

Pearl Malkin, as known as "Grandma Pearl" in her town, San Rafael, California, started making her bright canes at the end of 2012, when she turned 88 years old. Bored with her dull black cane, she decided to stick artificial flowers on. She soon created different canes to match different outfits. It took her less than an hour to decorate the canes with flowers, which she purchased from crafts shops in town. She bought the canes from local Goodwill stores.[1]

When Adam London, a grandson-like friend, visited her, he suggested she turn the canes into a small business. But, how? London, an enthusiastic entrepreneur himself, told Malkin about Kickstarter and helped her launch a crowdfunding campaign on the platform to raise $3,500 in seed capital to initiate her business, Happy Canes.[2] He helped Grandma Pearl create a video introduction and launch a Kickstarter campaign. With support from the contributors in Kickstarter, she planned to line up additional resources so that she could produce more canes. During a month-long campaign, 248 contributors pledged $5,039 to support her and bring Happy Canes to life.[3]

For her Kickstarter campaign, she prepared some alluring rewards to attract potential contributors. Contributors who had pledged $22 received a signed copy of *A Jewish Mother's Guide to Professional Worry*, a biography of Grandma Pearl, written by her son.[4] More engaged contributors who pledged $90, were rewarded with the book, a Happy Cane, and one voicemail from her. One investor pledged $500 and was compensated with a lesson for decorating canes and a four-course home-made lunch served by Malkin. The funds were used to create a new line of canes for her store at Etsy, an online marketplace for handmade and vintage items.

Happy Canes and the crowdfunding campaign gave Grandma Pearl her second heyday in life. Bringing enjoyment to other peoples' lives had always been the purpose of her life. She once performed as a standup comedian and volunteered for local communities. Crowdfunding revived her life once again.

One of the most famous crowdfunding campaigns for silliness is the campaign launched in 2014 at Kickstarter by Zach "Danger" Brown in Ohio for cooking his first ever potato salad.[5] Brown set up the crowdfunding campaign to raise $10 so he could make potato salad. Surprisingly, in 30 days, the campaign generated a viral sensation with raising funds of $55,492 from 6,911 contributors.

The campaign was initiated with a local newspaper article about potato salad that developed into a joke among Brown and his circles. The crowdfunding campaign was an acceleration of the joke, and Brown supposed Kickstarter would reject the idea and terminate the silliness. But, it didn't happen because Kickstarter loosened its rules a month before, allowing pitches seeking funding for campaigns to be posted on the platform instantly, without being reviewed by platform operators. Instead, over the first weekend of the campaign period, the pledges piled up. As pledges poured in, he was even invited out west by the Idaho Potato Commission. There he drove a tractor and harvested potatoes.

As expected, the campaign was not for a delicate creation of a famous or even experienced chef. Brown, the man behind the campaign, didn't have a recipe in mind or any specialties. Rather, he thought it would be better to provide potential contributors different value in addition to potato salad itself. The campaign's reward scheme provided everyone the opportunity to participate. He included silly things such as "I will say your name out loud while making the potato salad," and 2,084 contributors supported the campaign for this reward at $1 or more. And he owed 3,330 contributors "a bite of the potato salad."[6] Brown added the stretch goals and rewards as the funding went viral, including better mayonnaise in the recipe, customized T-shirts, a hat, and finally cookbooks. Pledges allegedly escalated after Brown offered those customized rewards, some with the slogan "I just backed potato salad" on them.

Brown spent a major portion of the funding on a local festival that he titled PotatoStock 2014 in Columbus, two months after the campaign's success.[7] Additionally, he created an endowment with $20,000 to the Columbus Foundation, a civic foundation aiming to end hunger and homelessness. He started the effort with funding from the crowdfunding campaign and intended to add more contributions from the participants at the festival. And two years later, Brown has finally kept his promise and published a recipe book that fulfills the final stretch goal of the crowdfunding campaign.[8] The campaign ended and may be forgotten someday, but he contributed to the community and created something that he could have never created without crowdfunding: a legacy left from the crowdfunding campaign.

Anything can happen with crowdfunding

As always, it is not adequate to treat "crowd" as a homogenous whole. The crowd consists of different types of people with distinguished backgrounds and characteristics. This applies to both creators, who initiate crowdfunding campaigns for different purposes, and contributors, who are sources of funding for those campaigns. In Kickstarter, for example, as of April 2019, more than 160,000 campaigns across the 15 categories have been successfully crowdfunded. The categories include film and video, publishing, technology, music, games, design, food, fashion, art, photography, crafts, comics, theater, journalism, and dance.[9] Indiegogo, similarly, but more comprehensively, classifies the campaign types into the three large themes, such as tech and innovation, creative works, and community projects, and 28 subcategories under these themes.[10] Although the classification systems may differ by platform, we can expect that diverse campaigns across themes and genres are launched and progressed concurrently. At the same time, with these diverse campaigns introduced to platforms, different types of contributors join the corresponding crowdfunding campaigns for fulfilling their purpose. Diversity, the second beauty of crowdfunding, sparkles when we have a more nuanced understanding of how different types of campaigns are posted on the platforms and how those campaigns link creators to their potential contributors.

Crowdfunding involves a diverse set of campaigns, from sponsoring rising cultural projects to investing in new business ideas and supporting local communities. Or, from another perspective, it covers a set of campaigns with different purposes, including creation of new domains, innovation in existing domains, and protection of disappearing domains. Because crowdfunding platforms are open to introducing diverse campaigns to the public, creators are likely to launch their crowdfunding campaign due to different motivations. They include, but are not limited to raising funds, connecting with potential customers, testing product concepts, or promoting product awareness. On the same vein, as crowdfunding platforms such as Kickstarter and Indiegogo typically post campaigns seeking funds in return for rewards of value in different forms, contributors participate in the campaigns with different motivations and expectation. They may expect a reward in the form of a tangible product or intangible experience. They may be intrinsically motivated to support and help a creator and his/her campaign without expecting something in return for the contribution. They may seek social connection and relationship with a creator and other contributors. More importantly, creators and contributors who participate in crowdfunding with diverse motivations and expectations behave in different ways on crowdfunding platforms.

Whereas the increasing amount of literature on crowdfunding highlights a broad interest in the phenomena, our conceptual and empirical understanding of crowdfunding is hampered by the many studies that treat the industry as one homogeneous whole. I here argue that to demonstrate the effects of "the crowd" as types of financial flows through alternative financing channels, we must understand the diversity of crowdfunding from different perspectives.

This chapter explores the diverse types of players in crowdfunding platforms hidden by the term *crowdfunding*.

What researchers have found so far

All types of players, creators and contributors, in crowdfunding platforms participate in crowdfunding for different purposes and reasons. Although the existing literature on crowdfunding tends to treat them as a homogenous group, which leads to a lack of understanding on diversity of crowdfunding, a strand of studies has tackled this stereotype by identifying different motivations and thus practices of players in the crowdfunding context.

Gerber et al. (2012) conducted in-depth interviews with groups of creators and contributors and identified their different motivations to initiate and support campaigns, respectively. For creators, undoubtedly, one of the major motivations is to "raise funds." They need money for different reasons, such as launching a new product and finalizing the editing task for a new film. But, money is not everything. In addition to raising funds, creators are also motivated to initiate crowdfunding campaigns to connect to (potential) contributors through a long-term relationship beyond the monetary transaction. This motivation is salient for those who pursue steadfast relationships with their contributors. Creators, in some aspects, seek validation of their idea and capability. Successful crowdfunding campaigns may enhance perception of crowdfunded ideas and thus a creator's ability. Contributors' beliefs in their ideas and capabilities increase when creators obtain public recognition of their campaigns through successful experiences. The effect of crowdfunding success on confidence can be remarkable among creators. In many cases, creators are motivated to engage in crowdfunding because crowdfunding helps them expand their reach through crowdfunding platforms and other social media. It is not only for sharing their works publicly but igniting a conversation about them and their works. Finally, some creators may participate in crowdfunding because they desire to imitate the crowdfunding success of others. We can observe how a campaign's significant success encourages other creators to attempt crowdfunding.

Contributors also engage in crowdfunding campaigns with different intentions. Corresponding to creators' motivation to raise funds, contributors often seek rewards from the campaigns in the form of tangible products or intangible service. Contributors also support creators, and their campaigns, for upholding values. They support the creators who are seeking values that they believe in. For example, contributors in crowdfunding platforms may want to advocate the idea of seeking alternative ways of raising funds to maintain freedom to create and distribute new things. Finally, some contributors may join crowdfunding to engage in a community where they want to belong.

In the same vein, two of my studies with colleagues on crowdfunding identified four different types of creators and contributors, respectively, based on their motivations to engage in crowdfunding.

A creator typology

Our study on creators empirically validated the existence of diverse creator types (Ryu and Kim, 2018). We conducted a survey of crowdfunding memberships comprising creators and contributors of the same campaign. The results of our study identified the relationships among creator motivations, project characteristics, and crowdfunding performance.

First, based on the literature review and interviews with selected creators and platform operators, we posited four creator motivations: monetary need, achievement, prosociality, and relationship building.[11]

Monetary need is a crucial motivation for most creators. It comes into play when raising financial resources for a campaign is indispensable. Creators are motivated to engage in crowdfunding because it offers an organized way to obtain financial relief from people in their networks. Crowdfunding is specifically helpful for creators who cannot receive funding from traditional financing sources. It allows creators to raise considerable amounts of funds through many contributors each pledging small and medium amounts.

Achievement motivation is a desire to achieve the goal or the objective of a campaign. A creator with achievement motivation engages in crowdfunding to pursue satisfaction while tackling a challenge or creating a new thing. Self-belief of creators increases when they experience crowdfunding success. In addition to the success itself, the number of contributors and amount of funds raised are often seen as indicators of the achievement.

Prosociality motivation is the will to benefit a society or a community intentionally. This motivation focuses on the goal of improving the well-being of communities and society. It is sometimes prompted by confrontations with social issues that need member engagement. Although some creators are motivated to achieve for themselves, some are motivated to serve others. Such creators show a strong wish to support others and are willing to prioritize others.

Finally, relationship building motivation is a desire to form associations with other people, particularly contributors in the crowdfunding context. Creators, in some aspects, pursue emotional interaction and social bonding. In addition to raising funds, creators are motivated to engage in crowdfunding to connect with contributors for several reasons, including a pursuit of long-term relationships and obtaining feedback. As most crowdfunding platforms offer online communication features, they allow creators to communicate with contributors during and/or after the campaign period.

Based on the four motivations for launching campaigns, four types of crowdfunding creators were identified, grouped into clusters, and labeled according to their characteristics.[12] They are fund seekers, social entrepreneurs, indie producers, and daring dreamers. We also examined the differences among these four types of creators, including contributor-perceived campaign characteristics and performance.

Fund seekers are entrepreneurial organizations that adopt less formal business-to-consumer funding, crowdfunding, over traditional business-to-business funding sources, such as VCs or banks. The results show that monetary need is their main motivation. They are also the oldest among all creator types, implying that they may be more experienced and skilled than the other types. It is not surprising that contributors in their projects were the most satisfied with their reward. This is also supported by the analysis that they recorded the highest average funding amount per contributor. The existence of this creator group indicates that crowdfunding is a new digital platform for providing funding sources and other opportunities for diverse entrepreneurial parties who have suffered from the asymmetric capital market.

Social entrepreneurs are one of the most suitable types of creators in crowdfunding platforms. The results suggest that the campaigns launched by social entrepreneurs scored relatively higher rewards and societal contribution at the same time, indicating the reason why they could achieve superior campaign performance. Interestingly, their campaign performance is competitive, even though they have the lowest monetary need of all the types of creators. In addition, they are younger than other groups. It suggests another role of crowdfunding in encouraging the community of young and enterprising social entrepreneurs (Calic and Mosakowski, 2016).

Indie producers represent a group of creators who seek the creation of new cultural communities. They mainly propose artistic campaigns in crowdfunding platforms, such as campaigns related to music, films, and plays. They launch their campaigns to satisfy monetary need and are driven by relationship building. Generally, they lack financial resources and aim to build an active community and strong fan base for their work. The results show that crowdfunding plays an important role as a platform for entrepreneurial subcultures and artistic communities. With crowdfunding, new artistic experiments can be triggered, as is illustrated by the trend that crowdfunding platforms and creators all over the world are largely found in the creative sectors.

Finally, the daring dreamer is a group of novices or lesser-known creators who are willing to be introduced on the stage through crowdfunding. They record the highest value in achievement motivation, whereas their campaigns are recognized by the contributors as the least feasible, trustworthy, or active. The mismatch between their enterprising motivations and less favorable evaluations from contributors indicates that their work may not be comparable in some aspects against the other creator groups' campaigns. Nonetheless, crowdfunding opened a new door to those (potential) creators and contributes to encouraging and promoting diversity in different creative sectors.

The results of our analysis suggest the multifaceted role of the crowdfunding platforms in boosting and initiating diverse entrepreneurial activities in different creative domains.

A contributor typology

For the contributor typology, corresponding to the creator typology, we conducted another set of surveys with a group of contributors (Ryu and Kim, 2016). Again, we started by identifying six major motivations of contributors to engage in crowdfunding campaigns based on previous studies on motivations of crowdfunding contributors and participants of other crowdsourcing practices, such as open-source software development: reward, interest, playfulness, philanthropy, relationship building, and recognition.

Reward motivation refers to the desire to receive something valuable in return for contributing to a campaign. It is the most common form of extrinsic motivation in the crowdfunding context. Most crowdfunding campaigns offer and promote rewards, usually expected outputs from the work. Potential contributors are exposed to and possibly attracted by those rewards.

Interest motivation is activated when contributors pay attention to something that suits their characteristics and preferences, which is a representative form of intrinsic motivations. In the context of crowdfunding, contributors are more likely to participate in campaigns they consider interesting and worth supporting.

Playfulness is the motivation shown when contributors engage in enjoyable or amusing activities through their participation. As we found in the case of the potato salad campaign, some crowdfunding campaigns provide different, fun activities for promoting contributor participation. Contributors are more likely to join those campaigns when expecting playful experiences.

Philanthropy motivation indicates a contributor's willingness to provide charitable assistance to the creators of a campaign out of concern for humanity. This motivation is similar to donor motivation in the charity context, but the scope of crowdfunding is wider than that of conventional charity campaigns. Although creators launch crowdfunding campaigns for different purposes, expecting support from potential contributors to obtain their goals, some contributors are willing to voluntarily support the creators and their campaigns.

Relationship buiting motivation relates to the connection between a contributor and the campaign creator. This motivation corresponds to the creators' relationship building motivation. This set of motivations shows a role of crowdfunding in forming, and boosting communities across the domains. Crowdfunding platforms and campaigns posted on the platforms facilitate the connection of the contributors to the creators and other contributors who may support the same campaign.

Finally, recognition motivation, another type of social motivation, refers to a contributor's social desire to be acknowledged by other people. This is also known as "image motivation." Contributors who are driven by this motivation pursue prestige and respect within the community. Most crowdfunding platforms open campaign progress and activities to the public, and those activities can be readily shared on social media. In this regard, participation in crowdfunding campaigns could be a suitable way to boast about their contributions and influence.

We then analyzed the characteristics of crowdfunding contributors by conducting a cluster analysis, which identified four types of contributors on crowdfunding platforms: reward hunter, angelic backer, avid fan, and tasteful hermit. We also examined the differences and relationships among these four types of contributors regarding their demographic information, personality,[13] and funding behavior, grouped into clusters and labeled according to their characteristics.

First, contrast between the angelic backer and reward hunter types has important implications. Reward hunters are motivated by the reward they expect from contributing to a campaign, whereas angelic backers are mainly driven by philanthropy motivation. Angelic backers are older than reward hunters, indicating that older people are more likely to participate in crowdfunding with philanthropic intention. Angelic backers score relatively high on agreeableness and low on openness, supporting that they participate in projects with generous intentions rather than to pursue their own interests or admire innovation; they tend to pledge for charity or for films and plays. Reward hunters exhibit the opposite traits – low agreeableness and high openness. They fund art and design and game projects, which offer relatively high-value rewards. This difference is reconfirmed in their funding behaviors. Angelic backers tend to pledge smaller amounts of money earlier for larger campaigns, whereas reward hunters pledge later for smaller campaigns. These differences show that angelic backers are similar to donors who join altruistic campaigns and that reward hunters resemble investors who expect reasonable returns from their investment. (See Chapter 3 for better understanding the differences between donors and investors.)

Avid fans comprise the most passionate contributor group. They recorded the highest values in most motivations. These results may be related to their personalities: Avid fans are the most open, conscientious, extroverted, and agreeable contributors. Their enthusiasm is reflected in the amount of funding they provide, which is the highest among the four types of contributors. As crowdfunding natives, they embody the coexistence of the two opposite motivations, philanthropy and reward. Avid fans are similar to members of a brand community, in which customers are deeply engaged with a brand by participating in many brand activities. Similarly, they also deeply involve themselves in campaigns to satisfy their needs of connection to creators they support and other contributors with common interests.

Tasteful hermits are in a special position. They support crowdfunding campaigns as actively as avid fans, with higher reward, interest, and playfulness motivations, but they have lower social motivations, such as relationship building and recognition. That being said, they are found to possess introverted natures and disagreeable traits. This type of contributor plays an important role in supporting different types of crowdfunding campaigns through quiet but steady contributions. Considering the variety-seeking nature of digital natives, retaining and expanding this type of contributor require platform operators to propose a diversity of campaigns.

Creator–contributor match

We further examined the matching between creators and contributors in crowdfunding platforms. Based on a cross tabulation analysis with the pairs of creator and contributor types,[14] we identified how each contributor type is more corresponding and thus contributing to different creator types. The results show angelic backers are more likely to be attracted by social entrepreneurs while less responsive to the campaigns launched by indie producers. It clearly indicates the strong connection between two groups of creators and contributors through prosocial intentions. In contrast, reward hunters love to participate in campaigns of indie producers while avoiding the campaigns of social entrepreneurs. Tasteful hermits prefer campaigns of fund seekers while tending to be less responsive to the other types of campaigns. It is interesting that both tasteful hermits and fund seekers possess less social motivation, and thus they are more likely to interchange value with each other with limited social interaction, which satisfies both. Avid fans show no specific preference, which confirms their favorable attitude toward overall crowdfunding campaigns. The significant relationships between creator and contributor types are highlighted in Table 6.1.

Table 6.1 Creator–contributor type match

		Creator Type			
		1. Daring Dreamer	2. Social Entrepreneur	3. Fund Seeker	4. Indie Producer
Contributor Type	1. Angelic Backer	▓	■		
	2. Reward Hunter			▓	■
	3. Avid Fan	▓	▓	▓	▓
	4. Tasteful Hermit	▓		■	

Note: Darker color indicates a stronger positive relationship between creator and contributor types.

Our results also suggest the importance of crowdfunding campaign creators' use of effective targeting strategies. Depending on the characteristics of their campaigns, creators must target the right contributor groups in the appropriate sequence. For example, for campaigns with a philanthropic orientation, creators are expected to first find and focus on angelic backers then on avid fans and tasteful hermits; reward hunters may not be the best target for those types of campaigns. For campaigns based on novel and innovative ideas, the best approach is to concentrate on avid fans and tasteful hermits first. When the funding goal is nearly met, reward hunters can then be attracted. Or, in the early stages, first-come-first-served rewards, offering a limited number of rewards with relatively lower prices, may be designed to attract reward hunters.

Different characteristics across campaign types

Diversity of crowdfunding campaigns can be portrayed in different ways. In our study on the creator typology, we further examined how these different motivations affect campaign characteristics perceived by contributors (Ryu and Kim, 2018).

On the basis of three generic criteria for VC investments (i.e., concept, management, returns), as proposed by Fried and Hisrich (1994), we suggest the following three dimensions of criteria for evaluating the characteristics of a crowdfunding campaign: concept, creator, and returns. We then construct the six campaign characteristics based on the three dimensions: novelty and societal contribution (of concept), trustworthiness and activeness (of creators), and feasibility and reward value (of returns).

Novelty refers to the degree to which a campaign's ideas and objectives are new and original (Koslow et al., 2003). In the crowd participation context, novelty is important for promoting the participation of competitive users (Leimeister et al., 2009). For VCs pursuing high-risk and high-return strategies, novelty plays an essential role in investment decisions (Hisrich and Jankowicz, 1990).

For crowdfunding campaigns, novelty also plays a key role because it draws the curiosity and interest of potential contributors. A crowdfunding campaign perceived as innovative or unprecedented can gain public attention, whereas tedious campaigns are ignored.

Societal contribution is the degree to which a campaign has positive effects on communities or society (Reynolds, 1987). The charity-related nature of crowdfunding plays an important role when contributors determine their pledges (Belleflamme et al., 2014). This characteristic is essential to charity projects and strongly influences the participants of crowd-driven projects. As the crowdfunding mechanism is mainly based on collective behavior, a campaign associated with social causes or movements can expect more fundraising momentum.

Trustworthiness is a vital criterion determining contributors' attitudes toward creators and their campaigns (Belanger et al., 2002). Similar to the criterion that VCs use to appraise venture founders (Fried and Hisrich, 1994), trustworthiness refers to the extent to which creators deserve to be viewed as reliable and worthy of contributors' confidence (Sheinin et al., 2011).

Activeness indicates the level of a creator's enterprising attitude (Koh and Kim, 2003). This characteristic is required of venture founders who need to show their diligence (Fried and Hisrich, 1994). Along with trustworthiness, activeness can play an important role in lowering the perceived risk for potential crowdfunding contributors. This is because information on creators is less available, whereas information on funding progress is salient and easily available (Burtch et al., 2013).

Feasibility, from the perspective of returns, reflects the possibility of a campaign being accomplished as promised, and it is a requisite for persuading down-to-earth contributors (Krueger, 1993). Estimating the possibility of success is an indispensable process for investors (Tversky and Kahneman, 1974; Macmillan et al., 1985).

Reward value in return for funding is another standard used to assess the attractiveness of a campaign. An important obligation of creators is to design suitable rewards for contributors and to deliver them promptly. Similar to feasibility, reward value is the dominant index (i.e., expected return on investment) that leads to a decision of whether to make an investment (Fried and Hisrich, 1994). But, crowdfunding contributors do not care solely about financial returns, unlike traditional investors, and they may rely on different-quality information when making decisions (Lin et al., 2013; Liu et al., 2015).

Next, we examined how contributors' perceptions of campaign characteristics differ from cluster to cluster.

The campaigns of social entrepreneurs were perceived as the most significant contributions to society, whereas those of indie producers were perceived least significant. Social entrepreneurs launch crowdfunding campaigns from prosocial motivations; therefore, their campaigns are intended to contribute to society. Contributors might support these campaigns with a wish to participate in that contribution. The result shows that crowdfunding can lead to a new avenue for social innovation by connecting a group of creators with prosocial motivation and their potential contributors. This is possible because crowdfunding allows contributors to contribute a small amount of money and support societally meaningful campaigns; crowdfunding has gained significance with the failure of the traditional charity model to attract sufficient creative ideas and donors.

The campaigns of indie producers tend to focus on the producers' purposes and benefits; therefore, their contribution to society may be marginal. Thus, contributors in those campaigns might be motivated by other characteristics such as expected rewards or relational features of the campaigns.

Daring dreamers were recognized as the least trustworthy type and the least active among all creator groups. Their campaigns were also considered less feasible than the campaigns of social entrepreneurs. The high achievement motivation of daring dreamers might condition contributor perceptions toward their campaigns. As they are novice creators, potential contributors might perceive their campaigns as less trustworthy and feasible. Interestingly, even with their higher relationship building motivation, they were considered the least active creator group. This suggests the perception that their motivation may not turn into executable plans because they lack experience and expertise.

Finally, the contributors of fund seekers' campaigns perceived that the rewards they received were the most valuable. As fund seekers launch their campaigns solely due to monetary need, they might seriously consider a value exchange with potential contributors. Again, as they are the oldest group, they may be the most highly experienced. The existence of this type of creators confirms that crowdfunding plays a substantial role in financing diverse campaigns that have been neglected by institutional investors and thus had difficulties fundraising for survival or growth.

Overall, the results show that creators' motivations play important roles in forming the characteristics of the crowdfunding campaigns they launch.

Wherever diversity matters

Crowdfunding plays a role in places wherever diversity matters. Crowdfunding can salvage something valuable but disappearing for various reasons. For example, it appears that new creators working for independent bookstores and publishing are fully utilizing crowdfunding.[15] When looking at some of the top crowdfunding platforms, such as Kickstarter, Indiegogo, and Patreon, considerable portions of the campaigns are particularly for those funding books, comics, independent publishers, and bookstores. Vina Castillo, Natalie Noboa, and Holly Nikodem launched a crowdfunding campaign at Kickstarter for saving the Queens Bookshop, an independent bookstore in Queens, New York.[16] The three of them met while working at the Barnes & Noble near the Queens Bookshop. They all eventually went their separate ways, but when they heard that the store was closing at the end of 2015, they decided to reunite to save this beloved local bookstore. The campaign successfully secured the goal amount with 831 contributors pledging $72,360.

Independent bookstores are getting squeezed from multiple pressures, including competition from online bookstores, for example, Amazon and new technology such as e-books and smartphones. People appear to be reading fewer books.[17] This is actually a long-term trend, coming from the introduction of television. The result is disappearing independent bookstores across countries and cities. For example, in 1950, Manhattan had 386 bookstores; by 2015, the number was down to 106.[18]

Alan Beatts founded Borderlands Books in San Francisco in 1997,[19] and for almost two decades the independent bookstore, which specializes in fantasy, science fiction, horror, and mystery, has weathered challenges from Barnes & Noble, Amazon, and e-books. But when the city passed a law raising its minimum wage to $15 per hour by 2018, Beatts announced he was closing shop.[20] Actually, he supports the new law – although he wishes there was an exemption for small businesses like his – and thinks it will probably be good for the city. But the reality is that his bookstore is one business that simply isn't profitable enough to pay higher wages. Yet, he came up with a plan. He announced that the bookstore could stay open if it would get the help of 300 contributors, each paying $100 a year. Hundreds of supporters have signed up, raising enough money to keep the store open and even allowing him to expand.

Borderlands isn't the only independent bookstore to benefit from crowdfunding.[21] Singularity & Co was founded from a Kickstarter campaign to preserve vintage science-fiction titles that had fallen out of print.[22] They ended up raising far more than they asked for and decided to use the extra cash to open their own shop in August 2012.[23]

A publishing company also offers a new tool to indie bookstores: crowdfunded imprints.[24] Inkshares, a hybrid crowdfunding and publishing house launched a new project in which independent bookstores are given imprints on its platform.[25] An imprint on Inkshares is called a Collection, and only books that reach a specific pre-order goal get published, sparing bookstores any financial risk. With the Collection feature, any indie bookseller can add an Inkshares project to their Collection, so long as the author consents. In return for championing these books to help them hit their pre-order goal, a book would then be published under that bookseller's brand, and the bookseller can earn royalties from that book's sales. This allows a bookstore to publish without any financial risk, deepens ties with their local writer community, and for books that sell well, creates a potentially meaningful revenue stream because these books would be distributed nationwide. The company takes care of marketing, design, and distribution through Ingram, a large service provider for the publishing industry.

It is still hard for those independent bookstores and publishers to compete with online and off-line giants such as Barnes & Noble and Amazon on prices or assortment. Although crowdfunding could not support independent bookstores and publishers to provide Amazon's low prices or Barnes & Noble's wide selection or physical space, they have kept neighborhood stores in neighborhoods. For sure, crowdfunding isn't just about money.[26] Local bookstores could offer experiences that can't be replicated online, such as browsing bookshelves, meeting local fans, and attending live readings. The success of crowdfunding campaigns seems to support a community, which is definitely a role that crowdfunding plays for those creators. We will discuss more on the role of crowdfunding in building up and supporting a community in Chapter 8.

Key takeaways

- In the crowdfunding context, the crowd consists of different types of people with distinguished backgrounds and characteristics. This applies to both creators, who initiate crowdfunding campaigns for different purposes, and contributors, who are sources of funding for those campaigns. Because of the diversity, anything can happen with crowdfunding.
- Crowdfunding involves a diverse set of campaigns, from promoting rising creative projects to investing in new business ideas and supporting local communities. It also covers a set of campaigns with different purposes, including creation of new domains, innovation in the existing domains, and protection of disappearing domains.
- Contributors also participate in crowdfunding for different purposes and reasons. It is important for creators to use effective targeting strategies depending on the characteristics of their campaigns. Creators must target suitable contributor groups in the appropriate sequence.
- Crowdfunding plays its role in places wherever diversity matters. Specifically, crowdfunding can salvage something valuable but disappearing for various reasons, such as independent bookstores.

Notes

1 www.huffpost.com/entry/grandma-pearl_n_2529351
2 They also launched a store at Etsy, an online marketplace for handcrafted goods in January 2013. The canes sold for $60 on Etsy.
3 www.kickstarter.com/projects/998024426/happy-canes-spring-13-canes-for-grandma
4 https://money.cnn.com/2013/02/20/smallbusiness/grandma-kickstarter-startup/index.html
5 www.kickstarter.com/projects/zackdangerbrown/potato-salad
6 https://money.cnn.com/2014/08/03/technology/social/potato-salad-crowdfunding/
7 www.theguardian.com/world/2014/sep/27/potato-salad-kickstarter-ohio-fundraising-potatostock-party
8 www.polygon.com/2016/7/17/12208840/potato-salad-kickstarter-cookbook-zack-danger-brown
9 www.kickstarter.com/help/stats
10 www.indiegogo.com/explore
11 Among the several construct dimensions proposed in previous studies to categorize motivations, we chose two: intrinsic verses extrinsic and self-oriented verses others oriented. The framework that includes intrinsic and extrinsic motivations in Self-Determination Theory (SDT) is the most frequently referenced. In SDT, a behavior is extrinsically motivated when performed to achieve significant outcomes, whereas a behavior is intrinsically motivated when performed for inherent

joy or playfulness. The other frequently cited dichotomy distinguishes between two types of motivation: self-oriented and others oriented. Self-oriented motivation is associated with the uncomplicated link between an actor and an object (i.e., task, product), whereas others-oriented motivation is concerned with an actor's social and emotional relationships with the object.

12 Through the two-step approach, we received 729 responses (617 contributors of 144 campaigns and 112 creators). Of the total responses, 62 responses (58 investors and four creators) were eliminated from the sample due to incomplete responses, such as missing values, resulting in 667 responses of 559 contributors, from 131 campaigns, and 108 creators. Of these, 362 contributors and 45 creators were matched, meaning that 45 campaigns had both creator and investor responses, whereas the others had responses from only one side.

13 The Big-Five Model is used to investigate personality. This model has been widely acknowledged as the standard for measuring different personality traits and has been used consistently in studies in conjunction with methodologies such as interviews, self-description, and observation. The components are openness to experience, conscientiousness, extraversion, agreeableness, and neuroticism. Openness (to experience) refers to flexibility in thinking and tolerance of new ideas. Conscientiousness indicates organization, persistence, and motivation in goal-directed behavior. Extraversion refers to the degree to which people are sociable, gregarious, and ambitious. Agreeableness indicates the degree to which a person exhibits compassion and an interpersonal orientation. Neuroticism is emotional instability, insecurity, anxiety, and hostility. This trait is reflected in a negative attitude.

14 Cross-tabulation analysis groups data points to understand the correlation between different groups. It also shows how correlations change from one subject grouping to another. It is usually used in statistical analysis to find patterns, trends, and probabilities within data. We conducted the cross-tabulation analysis based on the 319 pairs of creator (i.e., campaign)–contributor match. A high value of Pearson's chi-square (i.e., 19.379, $p < 0.01$) indicates an association between two sides of clusters, which implies a certain type of contributor prefers suitable campaigns rather than others.

15 www.forbes.com/sites/jenniferbaker/2016/06/07/how-viable-is-crowdfunding-for-book-entrepreneurs/#7c945ec9298d
16 www.kickstarter.com/projects/1844468864/lets-bring-a-bookshop-back-to-queens-ny
17 www.theguardian.com/books/2019/mar/04/why-are-new-yorks-bookstores-disappearing
18 https://gothamist.com/2015/01/30/rip_nyc_bookstores.php
19 https://borderlands-books.com
20 www.wired.com/2015/04/geeks-guide-crowdfunding-bookstores/
21 www.theatlantic.com/entertainment/archive/2013/08/if-you-want-keep-book stores-donate-kickstarter/312281/
22 www.kickstarter.com/projects/singularityco/singularity-and-co
23 www.wired.com/2015/04/geeks-guide-crowdfunding-bookstores/
24 www.fastcompany.com/3047677/this-publishing-startup-wants-to-crowdfund-books-for-indie-bookstores
25 www.inkshares.com
26 www.publishersweekly.com/pw/by-topic/industry-news/bookselling/article/61545-beyond-the-bank-bookstores-and-alternative-funding.html

References

Belanger, F., Hiller, J. S. & Smith, W. J. 2002. Trustworthiness in Electronic Commerce: The Role of Privacy, Security, and Site Attributes. *Journal of Strategic Information Systems*, 11, 245–270.

Belleflamme, P., Lambert, T. & Schwienbacher, A. 2014. Crowdfunding: Tapping the Right Crowd. *Journal of Business Venturing*, 29, 585–609.

Burtch, G., Ghose, A. & Wattal, S. 2013. An Empirical Examination of the Antecedents and Consequences of Contribution Patterns in Crowd-Funded Markets. *Information Systems Research*, 24, 499–519.

Calic, G. & Mosakowski, E. 2016. Kicking Off Social Entrepreneurship: How A Sustainability Orientation Influences Crowdfunding Success. *Journal of Management Studies*, 53, 738–767.

Fried, V. H. & Hisrich, R. D. 1994. Toward a Model of Venture Capital Investment Decision Making. *Financial Management*, 23, 28–37.

Gerber, E. M., Hui, J. S. & Kuo, P. 2012. Crowdfunding: Why People Are Motivated to Post and Fund Projects on Crowdfunding Platforms. *Proceedings of the International Workshop on Design, Influence, and Social Technologies: Techniques, Impacts and Ethics*. Northwestern University, Evanston, IL. Retrieved on March.

Hisrich, R. D. & Jankowicz, A. D. 1990. Intuition in Venture Capital Decisions: An Exploratory Study Using a New Technique. *Journal of Business Venturing*, 5, 49–62.

Koh, J. & Kim, Y-G. 2003. Sense of Virtual Community: A Conceptual Framework and Empirical Validation. *International Journal of Electronic Commerce*, 8, 75–94.

Koslow, S., Sasser, S. L. & Riordan, E. A. 2003. What Is Creative to Whom and Why? Perceptions in Advertising Agencies. *Journal of Advertising Research*, 43, 96–110.

Krueger, N. F. 1993. The Impact of Prior Entrepreneurial Exposure on Perceptions of New Venture Feasibility and Desirability. *Entrepreneurship Theory and Practice*, 18, 5–21.

Leimeister, J. M., Huber, M., Bretschneider, U. & Krcmar, H. 2009. Leveraging Crowdsourcing: Activation-Supporting Components for IT-based Ideas Competition. *Journal of Management Information Systems*, 26, 197–224.

Lin, M., Prabhala, N. R. & Viswanathan, S. 2013. Judging Borrowers by the Company They Keep: Friendship Networks and Information Asymmetry in Online Peer-to-Peer Lending. *Management Science*, 59, 17–35.

Liu, D., Brass, D. J., Lu, Y. & Chen, D. 2015. Friendships in Online Peer-to-Peer Lending: Pipes, Prisms, and Relational Herding. *MIS Quarterly*, 39, 729–742.

Macmillan, I. C., Siegel, R. & Narasimha, P. N. S. 1985. Criteria Used by Venture Capitalists to Evaluate New Venture Proposals. *Journal of Business Venturing*, 1, 119–128.

Reynolds, P. D. 1987. New Firms: Societal Contribution Versus Survival Potential. *Journal of Business Venturing*, 2, 231–246.

Ryu, S. & Kim, Y-G. 2016. A Typology of Crowdfunding Sponsors: Birds of a Feather Flock Together? *Electronic Commerce Research and Applications*, 16, 43–54.

Ryu, S. & Kim, Y-G. 2018. Money Is Not Everything: A Typology of Crowdfunding Project Creators. *Journal of Strategic Information Systems*, 27, 350–368.

Sheinin, D. A., Varki, S. & Ashley, C. 2011. The Differential Effect of Ad Novelty and Message Usefulness on Brand Judgments. *Journal of Advertising*, 40, 5–18.

Tversky, A. & Kahneman, D. 1974. Judgment Under Uncertainty: Heuristics and Biases. *Science*, 185, 1124–1131.

7 Balance

A new history of hardware ventures

Traditional sources of capital, especially financing for new ventures, prefer (or avoid) companies with certain types of products. For example, VCs have long neglected hardware ventures, which accounted for less than 1% of total investment each year from 1992 to 2011.[1] Any new venture possesses risk, but hardware ventures are particularly risky because they require more investment in facilities for production. Moreover, due to longer cycles of product development, expected time for realizing return on investment could be longer than non-hardware products. In addition to product development and production, hardware ventures also must master the logistics of supply and distribution chains. Because of those reasons, hardware ventures have suffered from disadvantages in financing for their earlier stages of business. Interestingly, however, crowdfunding is more favorable to and even prefers hardware products. Dominant beneficiaries of crowdfunding are those hardware ventures.

Palmer Luckey, a young Californian engineer, fell in love with the concept of VR when he was around 15 years old.[2] During his childhood and teenage years, he experimented with a variety of complex scientific projects. His passion to engage in virtual worlds led him to an enthusiasm with VR, which had not attracted significant attention of the industry for considerable time. In the late 1980s and 1990s, many companies attempted to commercialize VR hardware, but all of them failed.[3] Some products were too overpriced. Others didn't perform well. Most importantly, they were too early for their time.

Luckey's favorite thing to handle was early attempts at VR headsets. To learn more about VR technology, Luckey initiated a huge private collection of different headsets. Most of the collection was developed in the 1990s. He found his collection here and there, from industry clearance sales to government auctions. Turning 16, he began developing his own VR headsets. Not satisfied with the performance of the collections he obtained, he set out to build something better. Some designs were combined together from the collection; others were upgraded versions of the previous displays; others were developed entirely from the scratch. To fund these projects, he made money by fixing and reselling damaged iPhones and working part-time jobs, such as groundskeeper and computer repair technician.[4] At that time, he was attending classes at California State University, Long Beach, pursuing a journalism degree. In the meanwhile, he also worked as an assistant engineer at the Mixed Reality Lab of the University of Southern California, experimenting with VR and head-mounted displays.

During his research and development, he actively participated in an online forum on VR technology for sharing his idea and receiving feedback from experts. During his active participation, one day, Luckey found himself chatting with John Carmack, a cofounder of id Software and the lead programmer of Doom and Quake. Carmack found high potential in Luckey's project on VR headsets, turning it from a daring experiment for building VR devices in a garage to a special device that everyone in the industry was interested in. Later, Luckey dropped out of college to start a company. In June 2012, he founded OculusVR, later renamed to Oculus.

In August 2012, Luckey launched his Kickstarter campaign.[5] When Luckey first started thinking about developing a VR headset, long before he ever formed a company, he wished he could find a small group of enthusiasts, around 100 or more, to support his experiment. Then the endorsements from John Carmack came, and other industry giants joined to support his VR project. He set up a humble campaign goal: $250,000. The outcome was surprising. Within 24 hours, he raised around $670,000 from 2,750 contributors. Within three days, he passed $1 million.

When the campaign closed, 9,522 contributors had put in a total of $2,437,429, almost 10 times the amount that Luckey asked for. Depending on the amount of their contribution, contributors received the rewards, from a thank-you letter to their own prototype of the headset. Surprisingly, one more time, a year later, it was announced that Oculus was being sold to Facebook for $2 billon.[6] "I'm passionate about bringing games to the next level," Luckey told potential contributors in his original Kickstarter video.[7]

Facebook began shipping the Oculus Rift to customers in 2016.[8] It was actually not the first VR headset introduced to the market. Yet, at the price of $1,500 for the device, although it needed a computer to run it, it was the first VR headset that was sophisticated and remarkably inexpensive. It is also the first headset free of motion sickness. Oculus has developed a series of VR headsets since Facebook's acquisition in 2013, and Oculus Quest, a most recent standalone VR headset was expected sell more than 1.3 million units in 2019 according to a market research company.[9]

Balancing the biased capital markets

Crowdfunding performs as a stepping stone to balance the biased capital markets by financing the domains that have been neglected by traditional investors, such as VCs and banks. Crowdfunding plays an important role in creating a society where more people experience the advantages of capitalism.[10] Crowdfunding platforms distribute money to creators who have no connections. It is possible from contributions made by contributors. Crowdfunding has emerged as an alternative financing source. We see many ventures raise money from crowdfunding. This helps free capital from the pockets of the crowd and offers businesses a dose of growth capital.[11] It offers benefits to those with disadvantages in some aspects including but not limited to production type, location, and gender of founders.

As we discussed in the previous section, hardware ventures that develop physical devices have often struggled for funding because of the higher risk and capital requirements of hardware development over software. Moreover, in the past, hardware ventures could spend years developing a product that never ended up being favored or adopted in the end.[12] These ventures did their "testing" by recruiting users and taking small sample sets to evaluate product–market fit. Now, hardware ventures have many different opportunities today with the introduction of crowdfunding. It has dramatically transformed the opportunities for hardware ventures by taking the prototype to pre-sale before producing the product at large scale. Crowdfunding validates the product–market fit early in the development cycle before ventures spend millions of dollars creating something nobody wants.[13] It is also the most efficient form of marketing. It creates an informed community who then evangelizes. The main focus has been changed to creating a story that attracts attention and interest from potential contributors, and from there crowdfunding is used to build the products.[14] Crowdfunding campaigns can be helpful to hardware ventures in ways that go beyond money and marketing.

Traditional capital markets have been also significantly geographic dependent as the majority of investors are clustered in a few cities and regions. The private market of investing in growing businesses has traditionally been private and confidential. In 2017 three metro areas – San Francisco, New York, and San Jose, California – took about two-thirds of VC investment. Their share has actually increased since 2015,[15] driven in part by super-sized late-stage financing rounds for companies. Chen et al. (2010) examined the location of US VC firms' headquarters, branch offices, and investments as well as their investment success rates. Not surprisingly, VCs are heavily clustered in just three areas of the country: San Francisco/San Jose, New York, and Boston. More than half of all VC offices in the United States are located in those three metropolitan areas. Around 50% of all ventures funded by VCs are located in those areas, too. VC firms are concentrated in the regions where VC investments have been successful before. Those regions are in states with higher levels of economic status. VC-focused regions also have high numbers of patents.[16] Moreover, VCs that locate their headquarters in these three regions have a higher success rate than other VCs. The reasons are simple and straightforward. These cities naturally attract a lot of entrepreneurial talent as their ecosystems are better to support ventures. In addition, many VCs are present in these cities where their networks are reinforced. These indicate that the rest of the United States, a considerably large area, is underfunded.[17]

Interestingly, even though VC firms located in those big VC clusters perform better overall and they overwhelmingly invest in "local" ventures, the VC firms earn better returns from their investments in the ventures located outside their region. VCs prefer to invest close to their locations because they can more easily monitor their portfolios. They may invest in ventures located far from their regions only when the ventures are remarkably promising.[18] This indicates that VCs may have relatively lower evaluation criteria for ventures that are closer to them because such ventures are less expensive to keep in touch. In other words, ventures outside the regions of VCs may have to meet higher standards to secure VC investment and then are more likely to perform better.

Crowdfunding has the potential to address the bias and actually does in some domains, enabled by accessible online platforms, and opening up opportunities to the general public across regions and countries. An analysis on the comparison between VCs and Kickstarter shows the top five metropolitan areas captured 46% of successfully pledged funding on Kickstarter – still a relatively high share but much less concentrated than VCs.[19] The scale of VC investment ($75 billion in 2017 only) dwarfs successful Kickstarter funding ($1.5 billion between 2010 and 2017) though. Again, the VC-funded ventures located in the major, largest metropolitan areas accounted for 81% of all VC investment.[20]

But for some regions, crowdfunding plays a more significant role. Nine of the nation's 100 largest metropolitan areas have received more funding from Kickstarter than from VCs.[21] For example, Las Vegas, New Orleans, and Buffalo are among the six metro areas in which VC investment is less than 10 times the Kickstarter funding from 2010 to 2015. Local companies that launched through crowdfunding campaigns could also benefit from the connection to business-supporting services or access to additional financing. In this way, crowdfunding platforms could provide the opportunity for those regions to broaden their economic growth.

Last, gender bias in the capital market is another huge obstacle. For example, only one female founder gets funding from VCs for every nine male founders who receive investments.[22] Only 2.7% of VC-funded ventures from 2011 to 2013 had female CEOs.[23] Women are getting turned down for investment opportunities despite the fact that a study from Babson College found that women-led VC-backed ventures earn 12% more revenue than men-led ventures.[24]

But there appears to be one haven for women in tech looking for investors: crowdfunding platforms like Kickstarter and Indiegogo.[25] Statistics show that crowdfunding has a more diverse distribution by gender; 35% of campaign creators on Kickstarter are female compared to 18% of VC-funded ventures that have at least one female cofounder.[26] Women also enjoy higher rates of success in funding their campaigns across almost all categories except for games. The female founders, who were repeatedly turned down by VCs, are responsible for 47% of successful Indiegogo campaigns.[27] A potential explanation for these results is that women are better at articulating who they see as their contributors as an integral part of their teams rather than simply as contributors. Women have also seen increased rates of success on another platform: Kickstarter. According to a study on Kickstarter in 2014, female-led ventures have a 65% success rate as compared to 35% for fundraising attempts by men.[28]

Many crowdfunding platforms emphasize the importance of gender equality in the creative and innovative sectors. They put effort into supporting female creators and innovators. For example, Indiegogo is working with organizations like the Dell Women's Entrepreneur Network and Girls in Tech US to offer mentorship and consultations to selected female entrepreneurs.[29] In starting their company, Indiegogo's founders sought to create a platform that would remove some of those biases, unconscious ones based on gender, race, or class. Most crowdfunding platforms aim to put all enterprising creators and entrepreneurs on equal ground.

From the contributor side, it is a key ingredient in promoting gender equality through crowdfunding that an influential group of women helps female creators on their way in some male-dominated fields.[30] If female creators are able to access financial sources through crowdfunding platform, specifically where women are more likely to be potential contributors, there could be a leap in female entrepreneurship. It may offer more growth opportunities than in relatively traditional fields.[31] For example, Catapult is a crowdfunding platform dedicating to female-driven ventures and initiatives.[32] It aims to transform individual generosity into the power of shared, collective action by supporting girls and women working on the front lines for their equal rights. The increasing predominance of crowdfunding platforms may lead to more participation of women as contributors and to growth of capital flow into campaigns launched by women.

In conclusion, crowdfunding is expanding its role in offering opportunities for female creators and entrepreneurs to kick-start and develop their new and ongoing projects.[33]

What researchers have found so far

A strand of research supports that crowdfunding is addressing (or has potential to address) the biases of the current capital markets.

Addressing the imbalance across the industries

Stevenson et al. (2019) found that crowdfunding has the potential to address the imbalance of the capital market across different industries. They combined the investment data from both VCs and Kickstarter in the United States. They specifically divided data into two time periods, 13 quarters each before and after the launch of Kickstarter in April 2009. They assessed the shares of investment for VCs and Kickstarter at the industry level, focusing more on the period after the launch of Kickstarter. As supposed, VC investment is highly concentrated on certain sectors, like technology and healthcare. More specifically, internet, mobile, and telecom (39.40%); health care (25.11%); and environment, energy, and mining (10.78%) sectors obtained the major portion of VC investment. The industries obtaining the least investment from VCs are leisure (0.05%), retail and traditional media (0.27%), and food and beverages (0.66%). Conversely, crowdfunding, Kickstarter in their study, appears to fill the gap in those sectors. Interestingly, leisure, retail and traditional media, and food and beverages are among three of the top industries obtaining most crowdfunding investment. Overall, the results support that crowdfunding is filling the lack of investment in the industries that have been neglected by VCs.

Addressing the geographic bias

Regarding the geographic bias, Sorenson et al. (2016) found that crowdfunding, Kickstarter campaigns in their study, has been supporting entrepreneurial projects in different places that have typically been neglected by institutional investors, VCs in their study. Several cities with the largest number of successful campaigns, such as Los Angeles and Chicago, have not been recording significant VC investments, whereas VC investments have been highly concentrated in limited places located in Boston and Silicon Valley. Moreover, crowdfunding has been promoting the geographic stretch of VCs. Their analysis showed that a 1% increase in the number of successful Kickstarter campaigns in a year from the domains where VCs mainly focus on predicted a more than 0.10% increase in the number of VC investments in the same year. VCs could quickly adhere to a successful Kickstarter campaign as successful campaigns draw the attention of potential investors. They also found the association becomes stronger when the campaign domains are more closely matched to possible interests of the VC. The effects of successful Kickstarter campaigns on VC investment in the same regions have been enhanced over time. Relatedly, Yu et al. (2017) found that Kickstarter campaigns in a region correlate with increased angel investment. They used a lexical overlap method for separating campaigns of interest to angel investors from those of little interest. The results support that campaigns in the technology category have a strong and positive effect on angel investment in a region.

One of the most fascinating aspects of crowdfunding maybe the wider geographic dispersion of contributors. Agrawal et al. (2015) examined a crowdfunding setting that connects creators with contributors over the internet for financing early-stage musical projects. The average distance between creators and investors is about 3,000 miles, suggesting a reduced role for spatial proximity, compared to traditional financing channels. Distance still does play a role. For a single round of funding, local contributors tend to join relatively earlier and be less affected by decisions of other contributors. They showed this geography effect is driven by contributors who likely have a personal connection to the creators, such as friends and family. Although the online platform feature of crowdfunding may eliminate geography-related frictions, it seems not to entirely eliminate social-related frictions.

Addressing the gender inequality

Greenberg and Mollick (2017) analyzed 1,250 Kickstarter campaigns, dividing them into categories of those whose founders and contributors would be male (technology, gaming), female (fashion, children's books), or about even (film). They didn't examine any campaigns with goals lower than $5,000 as those campaigns might receive biased funding from inner circles such as family and friends. Across the categories, the campaigns launched by female creators were more likely to obtain their funding goals than those launched by their male counterparts. One striking finding is that female-launched campaigns had the explicit advantage in the category of technology, rather than female-friendly campaigns, which were often considered as less favorable to female entrepreneurs. It is surprising that female creators' success on Kickstarter was not only for female-related categories. The results suggest that crowdfunding's relative equality might arise from its ability to match female creators with a dedicated group of female contributors interested in supporting female creators in male-heavy industries. To validate this proposition, they conducted another lab experiment. They showed subjects Kickstarter campaign pages that already successfully funded, keeping all aspects of the campaign characteristics constant except for the name, gender, and picture of the creator. They constructed the identities of these founders, taking care to find ethnically similar people of average attractiveness and having them wear a normal gray T-shirt for their profile pictures. The results of the experiment confirmed that women who indicated an interest in promoting female entrepreneurship in male-driven industries were more likely to support female-led campaigns. This underlying mechanism shows why the female-led campaign for children's goods is less likely to succeed than a smartwatch campaign by female creators.

Relatedly, Marom et al. (2016) analyzed a Kickstarter data set that included 13,533 creators classified by gender, 898,491 contributors classified by gender, and contributions over $120 million in total, from April 2009 through March 2012. They found that women made up about 35% of the campaign and led 44% of the contributors on the Kickstarter platform. They identified that men on Kickstarter pursue significantly more funding for their campaigns and thus raise more than women. Rather, women enjoy higher rates of success in funding their campaigns. Women recorded a 69.5% success rate compared to 61.4% for men. Further analysis demonstrated what led to women's higher rate of success. Interestingly, it was not because of the women's more "humble" funding goals. The researchers found a positive correlation between the gender of the campaign and the percentage of the same-gender contributors. Kickstarter campaigns led by female creators were on average mainly funded by female contributors. Even though women constituted 35% of the campaign leads on Kickstarter, male contributors participated in only about 23% of campaigns among those female creators led. They also checked that this tendency for same-gender contribution is not due to the female entrepreneurs' tendency to focus on domains such as food and fashion. By conducting a follow-up survey among a sample of Kickstarter contributors, they identified that those male contributors who have a greater openness to gender equality were more likely to participate in female-led campaigns.

There tendencies are confirmed by the report "Women unbound: Unleashing female entrepreneurial," released by PwC and The Crowdfunding Center.[34] They analyzed more than two years of crowdfunding data from nine of the biggest platforms globally, and more than 450,000 seed crowdfunding campaigns. It affirms that female-led crowdfunding campaigns are more likely to be successful than male-led campaigns. It shows that campaigns led by women across the world, during the years of 2015 and 2016, were 32% more successful than those led by men across a wide range of sectors, nations, and cultures.[35]

Good crowdfunding stories for rebel girls

As we presented in the previous section, crowdfunding offers opportunities and resources for campaigns by and for women.

Elena Favilli and Francesca Cavallo, chief executive officer and creative director, respectively, of Timbuku Labs in San Francisco, are redefining children's media. *Good Night Stories for Rebel Girls* is a series of two children's books, targeting children age six and up. Each book features short stories about 100 real women who can be role models to children, especially for girls. Those women figures come from different eras, have different backgrounds, and are culturally diverse. Most importantly, they have a broad variety of occupations.[36] Examples of entries include Malala Yousafzai,[37] the Nobel Prize-winning Pakistani teenager who was shot by the Taliban in 2012, and J. K. Rowling,[38] the author of the Harry Potter series. Others are less "popular" but also achieved great things, like Irena Sendlerowa, a Polish woman who boldly saved 2,500 Jewish children from Nazi forces during World War II, and Lella Lombardi, the only female racer to score in a Formula One competition. It aims to tell young girls that they can grow up to be whatever they wish, regardless of what other people think.

Disparities in the representation of men and women in children's books has long been an issue. Books and pictures are crucial in defining how children see and understand the world.[39] By the time they are six, girls see themselves as less talented or "brilliant" than boys. The report suggests that both girls and boys age six tend to identify a "really, really smart" storybook character as a boy, not a girl.[40] Elena and Francesca believe that their emphasis on real-life rebellious women who challenged social norms gives an important message to children who frequently read about only fictional girls as historically women's achievements have been diminished in many domains. At the core of their company is this belief: that children, especially young girls, can be active, informed world citizens and overcome the challenges reality presents with imagination.[41]

The book was their modest follow-up to Timbuktu, their award-winning digital children's news magazine.[42] By changing the way people create the stories and giving the opportunity to more female creators, they are creating new stories. They found people are seeking stories with women at the center of the stage. They decided to launch a crowdfunding campaign for publishing the book as they believed that the crowdfunding model remarkably fit their mission and goals. In 2016, the first volume was recorded as Kickstarter's most-funded children's book, raising more than $675,000 (with an original goal of $40,000) from 13,454 contributors.[43] The second volume was also crowdfunded on Kickstarter, again breaking records on the website. It only took a few hours to smash the Kickstarter record for the fastest-funded publishing project in the crowdfunding platform's history.[44] A total of 15,475 contributors pledged $866,193 to help bring the second volume to life as the most-funded children's book in Kickstarter again.[45] With the second campaign, the team also released a podcast, so fans can listen to the adventures of the monumental women celebrated in the books. The first season features ten 12-minute episodes and a bonus episode for Kickstarter contributors.[46]

In addition to becoming the quickest and most-funded children's book in crowdfunding history, the book series is now an international bestseller in multiple languages. They have sold more than 1 million copies, and the books have been translated into around 50 languages.[47] They have been highly recognized as being an alternative to the stereotypical stories of girls or books primarily about male heroes.

After publishing the first volume, they regularly received messages from parents thanking the book's creators for helping make fascinating moments with their children.[48] They have a close relationship with their contributors and readers of the book through the crowdfunding campaign. Contributors have an intimate and emotional relationship with the book. They also received more than 500 suggestions from readers who wanted to see more women featured in the second volume.[49] In addition to creating a beautiful book, they also created an enthusiastic community of people all over the world who are eager for stories of women creating great things.

Here are more cases about ventures led by female founders with their hardware products, expecting the coupled disadvantages (female founder, hardware product) but overcoming them through crowdfunding.[50]

- Roominate, a Kickstarter campaign for dollhouses with working circuits, hit an unexpected performance quickly.[51] Roominate set up $25,000 for its goal amount and raised $86,000 to produce the orders. They had to redesign and change the process for making the design more modular, but they could handle these challenges. After the campaign, they raised some angel funding to start the scale of production to be a sustainable model.[52]
- GoldieBlox[53] is an initiation to get girls interested in building and construction. GoldieBlox founder Debbie Sterling wanted to test ideas for the girl's toy to encourage them to become interested in engineering. She has produced her first prototype and iterated the prototype until the toy resonated with young girls so that it could spark their interest in building and construction with the toy. She chose to go on Kickstarter with her concept to prove that someone loved the idea. She set up $150,000 for her campaign goal on Kickstarter and raised $285,000 in the end.[54] Through the crowdfunding

campaign, she could expand and develop her project to become more than an experiment.

No doubt that crowdfunding has come onto the scene and is a new tool for creators and innovators neglected by traditional sources of capital. Those "old" players maybe no longer be the only gate between creativity and innovation and financing. As a result, more creators and entrepreneurs have access to capital. Contributors have new exposure to different types of creativity and innovation. With crowdfunding, and its lower costs and greater liquidity, more entrepreneurial organization will be connected to funding. More ordinary people will participate in funding, and thus capital markets will all be better for it.

Key takeaways

- Crowdfunding performs to balance biased capital markets by financing domains that have been neglected by traditional investors. Crowdfunding helps unlock capital from the public and give ventures an injection of growth capital. Specifically, it offers benefits to those with disadvantages in some aspects including production type, location, and gender of founders.
- Hardware ventures, which have suffered from lack of investment, enjoy many different opportunities with crowdfunding in addition to the alternative financing opportunity. Crowdfunding validates the product–market fit early in the development cycle. It also provides an efficient marketing channel and supportive community.
- Crowdfunding has the potential to address the geographic bias, enabled by accessible online platforms, and open up opportunities to the public across the regions. Crowdfunding platforms could provide opportunities for economic growth for neglected and underfunded regions.
- Crowdfunding is expanding its role in offering opportunities for female creators and entrepreneurs to initiate and develop their projects. Many crowdfunding platforms make an effort to support female creators and innovators. Crowdfunding aims to put all aspiring creators and entrepreneurs on equal ground, regardless of gender.
- Crowdfunding is a new tool for creators and innovators neglected by traditional sources of capital. Thanks to crowdfunding, more entrepreneurs have access to capital. With crowdfunding, more entrepreneurial individuals and organizations will be connected to funding opportunities. Contributors also have new exposure to different types of creativity and innovation. More ordinary people will participate in funding.

Notes

1 www.wsj.com/articles/no-headline-available-1395077709
2 https://techcrunch.com/2014/03/26/a-brief-history-of-oculus/

Beauty of crowdfunding

3 https://techcrunch.com/2014/03/26/a-brief-history-of-oculus/
4 www.roadtovr.com/palmer-luckey-oculus-rift-interview
5 www.theguardian.com/technology/shortcuts/2014/mar/26/oculus-rift-facebook-fury-kickstarter-funders
6 www.theverge.com/2013/1/11/3867146/oculus-rift
7 In 2017, due to issues related to 2016 political contributions to Republicans and public support for Donald Trump, Palmer left Oculus.
8 www.vanityfair.com/news/2015/09/oculus-rift-mark-zuckerberg-cover-story-palmer-luckey
9 https://variety.com/2019/gaming/news/superdata-extended-reality-report-1203115821/
10 www.forbes.com/sites/philipsalter/2015/12/21/crowdfunding-and-capitalism-the-ties-that-bind/
11 www.forbes.com/sites/philipsalter/2015/12/21/crowdfunding-and-capitalism-the-ties-that-bind/
12 www.forbes.com/sites/hanjin/2017/09/13/the-new-path-to-starting-a-hardware-startup-lessons-learned-from-a-crowdfunding-approach/
13 https://spectrum.ieee.org/at-work/innovation/how-to-crowdfund-your-hardware-startup
14 www.forbes.com/sites/hanjin/2017/09/13/the-new-path-to-starting-a-hardware-startup-lessons-learned-from-a-crowdfunding-approach/#3d62c518d053
15 www.bloomberg.com/opinion/articles/2018-08-28/venture-capital-needs-some-geographic-diversity
16 https://sloanreview.mit.edu/article/understanding-the-geography-of-venture-capital/
17 www.forbes.com/sites/howardmarks/2018/06/10/how-crowdfunding-is-disrupting-vcs/
18 https://sloanreview.mit.edu/article/understanding-the-geography-of-venture-capital/
19 www.brookings.edu/research/hidden-entrepreneurs-what-crowdfunding-reveals-about-startups-in-metro-america/
20 www.brookings.edu/research/hidden-entrepreneurs-what-crowdfunding-reveals-about-startups-in-metro-america/
21 www.brookings.edu/research/hidden-entrepreneurs-what-crowdfunding-reveals-about-startups-in-metro-america
22 www.inc.com/glenn-leibowitz/women-of-color-get-02-percent-of-vc-dollars-this-startup-founder-plans-to-change-that.html
23 https://finance.yahoo.com/news/investors-melinda-gates-helping-vcs-113050297.html
24 www.babson.edu/news-events/babson-news/Pages/140930-venture-capital-funding-women-entrepreneurs-study.aspx
25 www.popsci.com/women-crowdfunding-success-kickstarter-tech
26 www.brookings.edu/research/hidden-entrepreneurs-what-crowdfunding-reveals-about-startups-in-metro-america/
27 https://go.indiegogo.com/blog/2016/03/women-entrepreneurs.html
28 www.theatlantic.com/business/archive/2014/08/women-are-more-likely-to-secure-kickstarter-funding-than-men/376081/
29 www.indiegogo.com/campaign_collections/a-celebration-of-female-entrepreneurs
30 www.theatlantic.com/business/archive/2014/08/women-are-more-likely-to-secure-kickstarter-funding-than-men/376081/
31 www.theupeffect.com/blog/women-social-enterprise-crowdfunding/
32 https://catapult.org/about/

33 www.forbes.com/sites/geristengel/2016/03/16/crowdfunding-is-a-female-founders-best-friend
34 https://medium.com/@atellani/women-on-kickstarter-and-the-power-of-gender-in-analytics-f9a73cb7e030
35 www.weforum.org/agenda/2017/11/the-tech-industry-needs-more-women-heres-how-to-make-it-happen-d1eec473-48cc-4801-bd40-dfba040b0e4a
36 https://msmagazine.com/2017/06/26/good-night-stories-rebel-girls/
37 www.bbc.com/news/education-39115031
38 www.theguardian.com/books/2017/dec/15/good-night-stories-for-rebel-girls-jk-rowling
39 www.fsu.edu/news/2011/05/06/gender.bias/
40 www.bbc.com/news/health-38717926
41 https://msmagazine.com/2017/06/26/good-night-stories-rebel-girls/
42 https://mashable.com/2017/06/20/good-night-stories-for-rebel-girls-volume-2-kickstarter/
43 www.kickstarter.com/projects/timbuktu/good-night-stories-for-rebel-girls-100-tales-to-dr
44 https://mashable.com/2017/06/20/good-night-stories-for-rebel-girls-volume-2-kickstarter/#c2G.WEufBSqb
45 www.kickstarter.com/projects/timbuktu/kickstarter-gold-good-night-stories-for-rebel-girl?token=07680cb2
46 www.huffpost.com/entry/good-night-stories-for-rebel-girls-is-back-for-volume-two_n_59493577e4b0cddbb009a5dc
47 www.thetimes.co.uk/article/good-night-stories-for-rebel-girls-a-revolution-at-bedtime-k8clzwlmv
48 https://mashable.com/2017/06/20/good-night-stories-for-rebel-girls-volume-2-kickstarter/
49 www.theguardian.com/books/2017/dec/15/good-night-stories-for-rebel-girls-jk-rowling
50 www.forbes.com/sites/women2/2012/11/17/kickstarter-funds-women-led-hardware-startups-everpurse-roominate-goldieblox/#2823bb26631f
51 www.roominatetoy.com
52 www.kickstarter.com/projects/369073015/roominate-make-it-yours
53 www.goldieblox.com
54 www.kickstarter.com/projects/16029337/goldieblox-the-engineering-toy-for-girls

References

Agrawal, A., Catalini, C. & Goldfarb, A. 2015. Crowdfunding: Geography, Social Networks, and the Timing of Investment Decisions. *Journal of Economics & Management Strategy*, 24, 253–274.

Chen, H., Gompers, P., Kovner, A. & Lerner, J. 2010. Buy Local? The Geography of Venture Capital. *Journal of Urban Economics*, 67, 90–102.

Greenberg, J. & Mollick, E. 2017. Activist Choice Homophily and the Crowdfunding of Female Founders. *Administrative Science Quarterly*, 62, 341–374.

Marom, D., Robb, A. & Sade, O. 2016. Gender Dynamics in Crowdfunding (Kickstarter): Evidence on Entrepreneurs, Investors, Deals and Taste-Based Discrimination. *Social Science Research Network*. Available at https://ssrn.com/abstract=2442954.

Sorenson, O., Assenova, V., Li, G-C., Boada, J. & Fleming, L. 2016. Expand Innovation Finance Via Crowdfunding. *Science*, 354, 1526–1528.

Stevenson, R. M., Kuratko, D. F. & Eutsler, J. 2019. Unleashing Main Street Entrepreneurship: Crowdfunding, Venture Capital, and the Democratization of New Venture Investments. *Small Business Economics*, 52, 375–393.

Yu, S., Johnson, S., Lai, C., Cricelli, A. & Fleming, L. 2017. Crowdfunding and Regional Entrepreneurial Investment: An Application of the CrowdBerkeley Database. *Research Policy*, 46, 1723–1737.

8 Connection

How the potato salad campaign turned into a festival

Do you remember Zach Brown's crowdfunding campaign for making potato salad introduced in Chapter 6? He launched his campaign to raise $10 on Kickstarter. However, this small online joke turned into a viral sensation. He obtained $55,000 from around 7,000 contributors. It started for fun at first, interestingly, but turned into a new community. After collecting the funding, he basically used a major portion to launch a festival for charity, named PotatoStock, in his town.[1]

At the end of the campaign period, he began work on PotatoStock. Contributors from more than 70 countries pledged. The top 10 countries that contributed to the project included the United States, United Kingdom, Canada, Australia, Germany, France, Sweden, Denmark, the Netherlands, and Switzerland.[2] Brown believed the blend of humor and seriousness behind his campaign was what attracted people and thus built a community. It also attracted sponsors for the festival. For example, the Idaho Potato Commission donated the potatoes used to make the potato salad. The Idaho Potato Commission invited Brown to Idaho, where they introduced him to a chef and recipes for potato salad. They escorted him to potato farms at the west side of the city. At the farms, he hand selected the potatoes right from the field and took them with him to make the potato salad in PotatoStock.

PotatoStock was created as a way to fulfill his obligation to contributors but also as a charitable event to benefit central Ohio. A fund, controlled by Brown, has been set up with the Columbus Foundation through which proceeds from the selling of food and alcohol concessions at the event will be invested. Every year, the interest earned will be paid to nonprofits targeting hunger and homelessness. At PotatoStock, with around 2,000 participants, portions of the snack are dished out to everyone, and they enjoy music and some fun games such as sack races. Brown and his supporters made and ran out of 450 pounds of potato salad. The potato salad was free for contributors, and there was a suggested donation for anyone who didn't back the campaign. Three hundred T-shirts printed with "Peace, Love and Potato Salad" were sold out in one hour. This festival raised a further $20,000 for the Columbus Foundation.[3]

Brown used his fame and recognition to build connections and help the community that he belongs to. His idea took on a life of its own, and he wanted to do something good. His campaign and PotatoStock served up more than potato salad. Throughout his potato salad adventure, the community came together to seriously support a bigger cause. It also seemed like people had a great time, which is a favorable bonus.

Crowdfunding for connecting people

Why did people give money to make potato salad? Why does anyone pledge money for any crowdfunding campaign? Whether you produce a VR headset, a smartwatch, or potato salad, people expect you to offer them value. One of values crowdfunding campaigns can provide to people is connection. Contributors support different campaigns for reasons that go beyond extrinsic rewards and instead relate to a sense of belonging. The internet is a big community, and people want to be connected to someone as we are social animals. People covet community, and crowdfunding can help. Crowdfunding has thus been proposed to represent a community wherein groups of people deliberately connect through a shared purpose or objective. Most crowdfunding campaigns are certainly founded based on notions that go beyond simple seller–buyer interactions. Thus, a sense of belonging is important for predicting a person's willingness to support a given campaign.

One of the biggest mistakes that creators of crowdfunding campaigns make is to ignore the aspect of community in crowdfunding. They miss a chance to foster a community.

Crowdfunding builds new communities not only for fundraising but also for new connections. It actually generates more value than pure monetary returns. Successful crowdfunding campaigns prove market demand. But, more importantly it builds communities of support.[4] Crowdfunding seems to connect creators to their contributors for short-term contracts, but it can also serve as the basis for lasting businesses and important innovations. In some cases, this community is defined by geography, but in others, personal interests in certain domains may delineate it. Or perhaps it is based on a common cause, problem, or global social or environmental challenge. In any case, it seems the nature of that community would be important to the success of a crowdfunding effort. Any particular crowdfunding campaign is likely to appeal more or less to its community of potential contributors according to their characteristics.

Crowdfunding by its nature is open – everyone with access to the internet is a potential contributor. Crowdfunding democratizes funding by providing direct access. It opens the ability to participate to many. Thus, it reduces the traditional role of gatekeepers and other concentrated groups that are limited in size and connections. Moving from an expert-centered process to a platform approach increases connections to each other and leads to more network effects. It generally results in successful outcomes for the campaigns and after-campaign performance as well. Creators can directly reach out to these communities to refine ideas and generate engagement.

Crowdfunding also offers creators an effective setting to develop social capital comprising digital social links with other individuals active in the same campaign and on the same platform as well. Specifically, crowdfunding gathers a crowd of individuals who share the same values and allows creators to carve out from this crowd a community ready to support them. This community arises from the intense exchange of information, comments, and advice that occur between the creator and his/her contributors during the campaign and once it reaches the goal amounts. Feelings of mutual identification and social norms of reciprocity build social capital relations among members of the crowdfunding platforms, leading them to show support to other members. This internal social capital, established through interactions within the crowdfunding platform, plays important roles during and after the campaigns.

The communities contributing to campaigns and platforms often come to feel a sense of belonging and ownership. Such a sense is quite positive because it can drive communities to create more value through promotional support, such as referrals to the campaigns and the platform.

Contributors may also view their contributions as the cost of membership in community. For example, reciprocity plays a strong role in crowdfunding, and contributors are more likely to support campaigns run by active members of the platform. Connecting creators directly to contributors transforms early-stage fundraising, making it more engaging and interactive. Crowdfunding platforms possess some of the features of online communities, such as shared goals and interests. If contributors perceive themselves as committed members of the crowdfunding platform, they are more likely to participate in its activities with pleasure. For example, individual contributors often share details regarding the campaign in social media, thus actively promoting it. They even engage with the creator of the campaign.

The notion of community is also reflected in the idea that contributors cocreate the campaigns. Contributors may be involved in campaign implementation in different ways. It could be sharing ideas with the creator, making comments on an update of the campaign, responding to other contributors' comments, or testing early prototypes. Such activities help increase the product quality and campaign performance. Contributors' enhanced connection to campaigns leads to commitment. Contributors with high levels of commitment will contribute more ideas and resources to the campaign. In addition, commitment will motivate contributors to advocate the campaign to others through online and off-line social networks. It expands awareness and helps the campaign reach its target.

What researchers have found so far

Crowdfunding as a cocreation process

In the crowdfunding context, communities of support play diverse roles by sequence of the crowdfunding processes. Hui et al. (2014), by a qualitative study on 47 crowdfunding users, identified five main types of roles conducted by members of those communities – "preparing the campaign material, testing the material, publicizing the project, following through with project goals, and reciprocating resources to the community." During each phase of the processes, they closely collaborate with other members by seeking and offering advice and spreading the word to their social networks to encourage people to engage in the campaigns.

For helping prepare campaign materials, they may provide some representative and successful (or unsuccessful) cases as references. They could offer advice on specialized skills and expertise required for conducting crowdfunding campaigns. That advice could come from general sources, such as websites, blogs, or personal contacts. The communities help creators test their campaign materials by providing opinions and feedback regarding both content and design. During the campaigns, members of the communities support marketing them by spreading the word and thus build a target audience group. After funding, they go through with the campaign goals and promised rewards by offering support for production and shipment. Finally, at the end of the loop, creators of the campaigns repay those resources back to the communities by providing advice and financial support so that a new group of creators can gain benefits from the communities.

Zheng et al. (2018), with the surveys of 277 contributors in a Chinese crowdfunding platform, examined how the cocreation process by contributors, their psychological ownership of the campaign, and their commitment to the campaign are interrelated. The results show that the cocreation of contributors participating in the crowdfunding campaign as a community member would lead contributors to achieve psychological ownership, which is a mental state in which they feel as through the campaign is "theirs." Creator activeness and social connection of the crowdfunding campaign are found to promote contributors' cocreation activity, confirming the communal aspect of crowdfunding. Finally, psychological ownership will in turn promote contributors' commitment to the campaign. To strengthen contributors' connection to a campaign, by providing cocreation opportunities, creators could promote their contributions to the campaign.

Role of social capital in crowdfunding

Considering this importance of community in crowdfunding, creators' internal and external social capital would be an essential component of any successful crowdfunding campaign. Zheng et al. (2014) examined the effects of three different dimensions of social capital – structural, relational, and cognitive social capital – on crowdfunding performance. Structural social capital, constructed by the degree of social network ties of the creators, is an influential factor affecting crowdfunding success. Relational social capital, measured by the obligation to support other creators in the crowdfunding platform, is also found to be an important factor related to crowdfunding performance. Finally, cognitive social capital, operationalized as shared meaning between a creator and contributors of the campaign, leads to more successful crowdfunding campaigns.[5]

Whereas some of the earlier literature on crowdfunding argued the importance of the external social capital of creators, represented by friends, family, and personal social networks (such as social media contacts), a strand of research focused on internal social capital, formed and developed in the crowdfunding platforms. Launching a crowdfunding campaign on a crowdfunding platform enables creators to leverage not only their external social capital but also a different dimension of social capital particularly developed within the crowdfunding platform as a form of community.

As we discussed, crowdfunding platforms are not only performing as intermediaries of financial transactions but also as connectors forming new relationships. Leveraging a sample of 669 campaigns in Kickstarter, Colombo et al. (2015) examined the effects of internal social capital, measured by the previous funding activities of creators in the focal crowdfunding platform on the amount of early contributions and the number of early contributors, which are dominant factors affecting crowdfunding success. Not surprisingly, the positive association between internal social capital and crowdfunding success is fully mediated by those two early crowdfunding performances. When compared to the effect of external social capital, constructed by social network ties outside of the crowdfunding platform, internal social capital is found to have a stronger influence on earlier contributions.

Relatedly, Skirnevskiy et al. (2017) developed a model to examine the effect of a serial campaign launch, another dimension of internal social capital in crowdfunding. More specifically, they assessed how internal social capital constructed in previous crowdfunding campaigns affects the performance of subsequent campaigns. With a large-scale sample of 19,351 campaigns on Kickstarter, supported by the survey responses of 106 creators, they found that internal social capital developed through track records in previous successful campaigns is positively related to more early contributions. Moreover, empirical evidence shows that earlier contributions from friends and family in the initial campaign are alternated with support from ardent contributors (of the initial campaign) during the following crowdfunding campaigns. Finally, more importantly, they found the spillover effect of internal social capital on external networks, spreading the word to their social networks outside the crowdfunding platform, and the effect is positively associated to the performance of subsequent campaigns

Buttice et al. (2017) tested more nuanced effects of internal social capital developed throughout the previous successful campaigns launched by the same creators. With the sample of 31,389 campaigns launched at Kickstarter, they found that the number of previous successful campaigns is positively associated to the probability of subsequent crowdfunding success. However, there is no significant effect of unsuccessful crowdfunding campaigns. But, if creators have already accumulated sufficient social capital in the crowdfunding platforms through different activities, such as supporting other campaigns, the effect of previous successful campaigns is rather weak. This indicates a potential that different dimensions of internal social capital may substitute for each other. More interestingly, influence of this type of internal social capital tends to be mitigated as time passes because it consists of a large number of connections with relatively weak ties and thus has a shorter life cycle. In the crowdfunding context, contributors are exposed to many alternatives. Without launching new campaigns in a timely manner, it can become outmoded.

From another perspective, the existing communities also play a critical role in crowdfunding. Josefy et al. (2017) examined the effect of the characteristics of community stakeholders on crowdfunding success. They collected a unique sample set of 176 crowdfunding campaigns related to supporting the local theaters across 38 states in the US.[6] All of the campaigns were launched on Kickstarter or GoFundMe, a platform to publicly raise charity-related funds, soliciting support from contributors both in their local communities and other more remote areas. They mainly focused on how cultural aspects of the communities, operationalized as the portions of artistic class, cultural class, and the number of historic places in the region, influenced the success of the crowdfunding campaigns. The results show that cultural aspects of communities could be a significant predictor of the crowdfunding success and raised funds. The success of crowdfunding efforts remains affected by the communities to which they belong. This is based on the assumption that although on the surface crowdfunding campaigns ask for funds, they will only receive them if the target community "buys into" the idea – if enough people in the target community see a potential benefit in a successful outcome of the campaign. Considering crowdfunding communities as communities of interest, campaign success is mostly driven by how a campaign matches with the cultural values of its target community.

Building a community before kick-starting a campaign

Although crowdfunding could build a new community, it also gains momentum from the existing communities. Do you remember the story of Oculus Rift in Chapter 7? Palmer Luckey, as a member of a VR online community, asked for help from his community members to support his Kickstarter campaign but also to assist in designing logos, generating campaign pitches, and improving technology.[7] Based on this support from the community, as we already know, the campaign that launched a couple of months later was a huge success.[8]

More than 90,000 fans of the *Veronica Mars* TV show, which aired from 2004 to 2007, opened their checkbooks to the tune of $5.7 million to make the film a reality.[9] The *Veronica Mars* movie campaign launched in Kickstarter met its goal within the first 10 hours and raised more than $5 million because the cult TV series had a loyal fan base hungry for more.[10] The Kickstarter campaign was set up for $2 million, but the contributions recorded almost triple the original goal amount. Seven years after the TV show was taken off the air, the *Veronica Mars* movie hit theaters and on-demand services thanks to its "old" fans and crowdfunding.

Three days after his potato salad campaign went live, Zach Brown appeared on the local news to promote his campaign. He had had 200 contributors at the point and finalized with around 7,000. What people often miss is that those first 200 contributors at the core of community have to come from somewhere. The truth is that most successful campaigns have contributors before they launch.

Creators are expected to identify and nurture potential contributors, share their stories, and get people excited. When their campaigns are launched, they already have a following with organically grown relationships.[11]

But how exactly do creators build their audiences before the launch if they don't have any existing community (like the Oculus Rift campaign), fan base (like the *Veronica Mars* campaign), or supportive friends and family (like the potato salad campaign)? Many crowdfunding platform operators and creators who managed successful crowdfunding campaigns shared how to draw the attention of potential contributors and build up a community in pre-launch periods.[12,13,14,15,16]

Build core circles of community

Every campaign revolves around strong relationships. Most creators may have a small community ready to support their campaign and help initiate the process of community building. These are family members, close friends, and colleagues. They are willing to support the campaign, no matter what it is, because they trust and believe in the creator. Building a community is all about relationships. These friends, family members, and colleagues are a key foundation of the larger community. Identify a smaller group of trusted supporters to join the campaign as a core circle. This enthusiastic group will support to spread the word within their own networks, initiating critical early momentum for the campaign. This early drive is indispensable for any successful crowdfunding campaign.

Moreover, thinking about a larger circle of early contributors would be helpful at this moment: A group of people standing just behind the closest circle will be targeted. They may be connections from alumni networks, associates from local organizations, or other professionals whom creators met at festivals. They can even be friends of friends who may have a shared interest in the themes related to the campaign.

Those circles would perform as a team of advocates committed to making the campaign real.

Define and reach out to a potential contributor community

Every creator is expected to identify and start engaging with groups and social networks that are related to the campaign. They can look into forums and conferences that other creators in the similar category belong to. They may share campaign ideas or early prototypes with those groups to receive feedback and start initiating interest in the campaign.

These members should be target audiences for the campaign. Your campaign could be about solving a problem, igniting their imaginations, or improving their lives. They may be early adopters of emerging technology or movie fans who are interested in a specific type of movie. Most importantly, they are a kind of people who are willing to contribute to the campaign, bringing a creative and innovative solution to the world. Every creator is expected to offer explicit value in return for their potential contribution.

For creators, participating in online or off-line crowdfunding forums would be good strategies. Crowdfunding forums are great places to communicate with the individuals who are also into crowdfunding. Potential creators can communicate with these like-minded people to find answers to their problems as well as seek for more information about how to design and implement a campaign. Another remarkable benefit of participating in forums is making the campaign visible in related domains. Creators could expect additional attention from the experts in the domains once the campaign is launched.

Setting up a list

Creating a list of potential contributors and their contact information is an indispensable step in running any successful campaign. A contact list is a great organizational tool that every creator can use to keep followers in touch with the campaign. First, many seasoned crowdfunding creators admit that e-mail is the most efficient and handy method for crowdfunding communications. Creators could collect email addresses, with some other contact information such as phone numbers and social media account information, in a single terminal. Once getting a sizable list, they will segment whether these potential contributors belong to fans, industry contacts, or acquaintances. Dividing the list into segmented groups will make it easier to refine and send customized messages later on. No doubt the pitch made to friends will be much different from the pitch made to a newcomer. Creators will need to refine not only messages but also communication channels for each of the groups identified. Knowing the potential contributors, and what will motivate them, will be critical in growing the community.

For snowballing the list, creators can leverage both off-line and online activities. They find local, regional, and national events that are related to the campaign, for example, some festivals, tradeshows, and networking events where they are likely to meet others who share similar passion for creativity and innovation. Creators should make sure to connect to those potential contributors by introducing themselves and their campaigns. Following up with new contacts immediately after the meeting is essential. In addition, creators should create a pre-launch landing page for their campaigns. The purpose of creating them is to get more email registration from people who are interested in the campaign before launch. Those who sign up are interested in finding more information about the campaign. They want to know when the campaign will be launched. That curiosity may turn them into remarkable leads for the campaign. Finally, creators are expected to make it easier for prospective contributors to stay in touch with them, which is demonstrated in the next section.

Regular and consistent presence to audiences

Once creators have built up their lists, it is time to regularly expose materials related to the campaigns to potential contributors on the lists before the campaign launch. Creators can choose a proper outlet to share updates about their campaigns. When launching a campaign, they could also share it through these outlets. It could be an official or personal blog, Facebook page, or e-mail newsletter. Creators are expected to choose a medium that will work for both them and their audience. No matter which outlet they choose, they should update materials regularly.

Newsletters can be a good way to engage more attention for the upcoming campaign. They can simply include more detailed information about the campaign and may add some exclusive deals. The primary objective here should be to increase credibility by helping those subscribers understand the creators' passion and devotion to the campaign. Creators should build trust for the campaign by leading more interaction before (and after) the campaign is launched. At the same time, creators can leverage social media to amplify their message and grow the audience. Creators should consider the benefits of empowering contributors to help distribute and promote the campaign throughout their networks and influence. Social media provides an opportunity to develop the campaign and learn more about what aspects of the campaign excite potential contributors.

This regular and consistent presence will help creators build a better bond with their potential contributors and followers and will lead them to the campaign as soon as it is launched. Consistency is key in choosing the number of postings on social media each week as well as the timing of posting, although they can adjust scheduling times and continue to check feedback from the followers.

Relationship, relationship, and relationship

Once creators build a community, they should understand that members of this community want to be connected to the creators and other members and moreover to be a part of making the campaign happen. This is the role of creators to cultivate those relationships. Creators are expected to be highly responsive to inquiries. They will answer questions and seek feedback. They also take suggestions and promote communication with their contributors. At this stage, the core circles of members will play their roles to rapidly expand outreach of the campaign by joining the communication as a unified and connected community. Most importantly, this community is a great asset. Creators should make a point to follow up and keep them informed at every stage of the campaign. The pre-launch phase is crucial for any crowdfunding campaign. Staying in touch is vital in these relationships. Many dedicated, hard hours are behind the campaigns.

Key takeaways

- Crowdfunding builds new communities not only for fundraising but also for connecting people. Successful crowdfunding campaigns form communities of support.
- The communities contributing to campaigns feel a sense of belonging and ownership. Such a sense drives communities to create more value through

supporting campaigns in diverse ways as contributors may view their contributions as the cost of membership in community.
- Creators' internal and external social capital are essential components of any successful crowdfunding campaign. Moreover, crowdfunding offers creators an effective setting to develop social capital comprising digital social links with other individuals active on the same campaign and platform.
- For any creator, it is important to draw the attention of potential contributors and build a community in pre-launch periods. After forming the community from core circles and potential contributor groups, regular and consistent presence will help creators build a better bond with the community. Most importantly, cultivating long-term relationships is the key by being responsive to inquiries, taking feedback, and promoting two-way communication with the community.

Notes

1 www.theverge.com/2014/10/1/6880201/potato-stock-kickstarter-potato-salad-zack-danger-brown
2 www.thelantern.com/2014/09/potatoes-unite-for-posterity-55k-kickstarter-campaign-finally-goes-from-spud-to-sald/
3 www.thelantern.com/2014/09/potatoes-unite-for-posterity-55k-kickstarter-campaign-finally-goes-from-spud-to-sald/
4 https://hbr.org/2016/04/the-unique-value-of-crowdfunding-is-not-money-its-community
5 Interestingly, Zheng at al. further compared the cultural differences between China and the United States by collecting samples from both countries regarding the importance of social capital in the crowdfunding context. The results show that the explanative power of the research model is stronger for the Chinese sample than the American sample. Moreover, the effect of obligation (relational social capital) has greater influence in China than the United States.
6 In the early 2010s, Hollywood studios decided to distribute their movies only in digital format. In response to the decision, independent and historic movie theaters were shocked as they lacked the financing to upgrade their projectors to digital ones.
7 www.kickstarter.com/projects/1523379957/oculus-rift-step-into-the-game
8 www.forbes.com/sites/ryanrobinson/2017/09/18/crowdfunded-side-projects-that-became-million-dollar-companies/#703185c53f1d
9 www.kickstarter.com/projects/559914737/the-veronica-mars-movie-project
10 www.cnbc.com/2014/03/12/kickstarter-funding-brings-veronica-mars-movie-to-life.html
11 www.entrepreneur.com/article/241262
12 www.forbes.com/sites/theyec/2018/11/06/how-to-build-an-audience-before-launching-your-crowdfunding-campaign/#1f2dbb1b53c7
13 www.forbes.com/sites/cherylsnappconner/2014/04/25/crowdfund-secrets-from-an-expert-who-raised-1-5m-in-6-consecutive-campaigns/#1afdf2fc718a
14 www.forbes.com/sites/theyec/2018/11/06/how-to-build-an-audience-before-launching-your-crowdfunding-campaign/#3a50c30753c7
15 https://techcrunch.com/sponsored/building-brand-communities/
16 https://news.communitech.ca/tell-a-story-and-build-a-community-indiegogos-ayah-norris-on-crowdfunding/

References

Buttice, V., Colombo, M. G. & Wright, M. 2017. Serial Crowdfunding, Social Capital, and Project Success. *Entrepreneurship Theory and Practice*, 41, 183–207.

Colombo, M. G., Franzoni, C. & Rossi-Lamastra, C. 2015. Internal Social Capital and the Attraction of Early Contributions in Crowdfunding. *Entrepreneurship Theory and Practice*, 39, 75–100.

Hui, J. S., Greenberg, M. D. & Gerber, E. M. 2014. Understanding the Role of Community in Crowdfunding Work. *Proceedings of the 17th ACM Conference on Computer Supported Cooperative Work & Social Computing*, ACM, 62–74.

Josefy, M., Dean, T. J., Albert, L. S. & Fitza, M. A. 2017. The Role of Community in Crowdfunding Success: Evidence on Cultural Attributes in Funding Campaigns to "Save the Local Theater." *Entrepreneurship Theory and Practice*, 41, 161–182.

Skirnevskiy, V., Bendig, D. & Brettel, M. 2017. The Influence of Internal Social Capital on Serial Creators' Success in Crowdfunding. *Entrepreneurship Theory & Practice*, 41, 209–236.

Zheng, H., Li, D., Wu, J. & Xu, Y. 2014. The Role of Multidimensional Social Capital in Crowdfunding: A Comparative Study in China and US. *Information & Management*, 51, 488–496.

Zheng, H., Xu, B., Zhang, M. & Wang, T. 2018. Sponsor's Cocreation and Psychological Ownership in Reward-Based Crowdfunding. *Information Systems Journal*, 28, 1213–1238.

9 Change

What changes crowdfunding is making

Simon Griffiths with his team launched a crowdfunding campaign in Indiegogo in 2012 to finance the first round of full production for their toilet paper business, spending 50% of profits to give toilets to those in need.[1] Simon's campaign was a remarkably effective way to get the word out about his new business. Simon raised 133% of his goal, $50,000, enabling the production run. The campaign also helped promote the growth of his business. As an Australian entrepreneur addressing a global issue, he pursued growth in different geographies and saw where his contributors came from. It helped execute his expansion plans. To date (as of November 2019), Who Gives a Crap has donated about $1.9 million to charity.[2]

Marcin Jakubowski, after finishing his PhD in fusion physics, was confronted with a lack of any practical skills to handle society's most demanding problems. Starting from scratch on a farm, he soon found himself entirely relying on others to repair and maintain his equipment. So he started fixing – and then producing – the equipment himself, sharing the plans on the internet as open-source blueprints. He soon realized, for building a village or a small town, it is expected to cost a lot of money and manpower. His solution is the Global Village Construction Set, a crowd-sourced manufacturing system.[3] This open-source product line of heavy equipment, such as tractors and soil pulverizers, has the potential to innovate the way we build villages. Launched by Jakubowski, the crowdfunding campaign raised $63,573 on Kickstarter.[4] The project has continued to expand its scale to the brink of revolutionizing low-budget housing, a necessity in needy parts of the world.[5]

These are examples of the ways crowdfunding is connecting social entrepreneurs, looking to make impactful changes to society to help people bring those ideas to reality.[6]

Here is another use of crowdfunding for change. Maria Zatko, an atmospheric researcher, was finishing her dissertation on ground-level ozone in 2014. She happened to learn about a remarkable opportunity to fill a gap in her research. Zatko, and the adviser at her university, found she could participate in an ongoing research project in Utah, exploring causes of abnormally high ozone levels during winter in the area. Zatko wanted to measure the release of nitrogen oxide from snow. But collecting the snow samples would require a month of fieldwork. Zatko had no research funding to cover the costs. She decided to try a crowdfunding campaign on Experiment. She raised $12,000, thanks to the 155 contributors who responded to her campaign.[7] The funds were essential for her to complete her PhD and even more important to bring her the opportunity for a new job with an environmental consulting firm after presenting the data at a conference.

Experiment, founded in 2012 under the name Microryza and later renamed, is one of the largest crowdfunding platforms for scientific research.[8] The platform allows investigators to create a profile and run a campaign to raise funds for a research project. Experiment pre-screens campaigns to ensure minimum standards regarding clarity of the research question, transparency, and researcher expertise. Requests for help typically focus on travel and lab costs as well as equipment and fees for publication and conferences. The most successful campaign, which is an extraordinary outlier, was led by Hollywood producer Gordon Gray, who pursued $1 million to develop treatments for Batten disease, a rare inherited disease.[9] It raised more than $2.6 million.

Another potential of crowdfunding for initiating change emerged from the journalism domain. Kickstarter launched a journalism category in 2014, linking with the *Guardian* to highlight campaigns with journalistic potential, as it had already done for sectors including films (e.g., with the Sundance Institute; see Chapter 5). Even before the launch of the category, Kickstarter had supported diverse journalism campaigns. One of the most representative journalism campaigns is Matter, a long-form digital journalism project co-initiated by former *Guardian* journalist Bobbie Johnson and Jim Giles, a US freelance reporter who has written for the *Economist* and *New Scientist*.[10] At Matter, as part of the article purchase, costing $0.99 to access for each article, readers could receive a "distraction-free web edition," an e-book version of materials for Kindle or iPad, and an invitation to a Q&A with the author. They took to Kickstarter with an original aim of raising $50,000 to get started but ended up raising $140,000 in total.[11] In 2013, it was bought by Medium, another new media platform company.

In addition to those "comprehensive" crowdfunding platforms such as Kickstarter and Indiegogo, there have been several vertical platforms focusing on news as well as journalism. Spot.us, a nonprofit news organization founded in San Francisco in 2008 and bought by American Public Media in 2011, was a representative player in the domain before it ceased operation in early 2015.[12] Its attempt to use crowdfunding to generate support for local news was unique and implicative for two reasons. First, it allows individuals to donate to individual stories rather than to the platform itself. Second, anyone can register as a reporter and pitch a reporting campaign for fundraising on the site. Spot.us, active for more than four years, provided an opportunity to think and develop the impact of crowdfunding on journalism.

In 2013, in the Netherlands, a new journalism experiment with the crowdfunding model was initiated. De Correspondent, founded by Rob Wijnberg, launched a crowdfunding campaign for innovating journalism.[13] The company intended to "unbreak" news, a goal that points both to its refusal of advertising and its editorial vision of avoiding the latest headlines but rather delivers to readers "the most important developments and underlying forces that shape our world," as its website states.[14] It succeeded remarkably in gathering more than 60,000 "members" who pay for its vision, raising $1.7 million in just 30 days and getting support from a Dutch investment fund. Readers are called "members" rather than subscribers because they are supposed to work with De Correspondent's journalists to provide their perspective on how to cover important issues.

Now, it is one of the most successful crowdfunded journalism company of all time, successfully raising $2.6 million in just 30 days for The Correspondent, a US version of its reader-driven news model in 2018.[15] They reached the goal of $2.5 million exactly 34 hours before the deadline. A total of 45,888 contributors from more than 130 countries joined. The median contribution was $30. Moreover, it attracted a number of high-profile contributors, including activist DeRay Mckesson and singer Roseanne Cash.[16] The launch of The Correspondent was welcome by journalists who were happy to see the company's successful reader-funded model expanded to the United States and other parts of the English-speaking world.[17] Under the crowdfunded journalism systems, journalists at The Correspondent will spend as much as 40% of their time talking to members about what they should cover. Their goal is to create the kind of reader–journalist community that many media firms have tried to build since the introduction of the internet – but has thus far remained ambiguous.

Making the world a better place

From those examples presented in the previous section, we could find potential, already realized to a certain extent, of crowdfunding to make the world to a better place by tapping vital but neglected domains. Social enterprises, scientific research, and journalism are remarkable examples. New attempts on crowdfunding platforms could be a seed for big change.

Social enterprises refer to all sorts of ventures that have a social mission as their primary goal, which "aim to be financially and legally independent, and strive to become self-sustainable by means of the market" (Lehner, 2013). Social enterprises possess a disadvantage, compared to commercial enterprises, in obtaining funds through traditional financial institutions despite all-time high interest in the field. This scarcity of funding represents an especially big problem in social enterprise because social motivation often takes first place over financial considerations. This does not satisfy the interests of traditional investors such as banks and VCs. Projects rooted in a social nature are unattractive to traditional investors because social goals sometimes conflict with the goal of profit maximization. This difficulty is escalated by fierce competition among socially oriented organizations to attract donations and government aid. Making it worse, the availability of these sources has dramatically decreased in recent years due to the recent economic crisis.

In this situation, crowdfunding has emerged to address the needs of social enterprises, in addition to other entrepreneurs, with limited access to traditional capital.[18] Pursuing crowdfunding as an alternative method of financing seems an appropriate step for social enterprises. Crowdfunding combines social values, social networks, and alternative reward systems. It answers to the financial needs of social enterprises as contributors typically do look at the ideas and core values of the campaign rather than business plans and expected returns. With those aspects, crowdfunding and social enterprise should match well.[19]

The situation is similar for scientific research. Funding amounts from traditional sources, such as the National Science Foundation, have shrunk dramatically. The grant-awarding process can feel arbitrary. The selection of those studies skews toward projects that possess fewer risks. In addition, most grants require scientists to provide proof-of-concept studies for their research, which makes it extremely difficult for more experimental projects to get off the ground. In the context, scientists are increasingly considering crowdfunding to support their research (Wheat et al., 2013). The power of science crowdfunding goes beyond financial rewards as it has the potential to connect science and society in a new, powerful way. Even though launching a crowdfunding campaign can be demanding and effort consuming as a conventional grant application, it is a promising alternative, particularly for researchers at the beginning of their careers who have a disadvantage competing for funding with seasoned scientists. Crowdfunding is also an alternative financing channel for researchers conducting research in the regions where funding opportunities are rare. It has the potential to tackle funding issues at the local research landscape.

The number of successful science-related crowdfunding campaigns is growing, and these campaigns demonstrate the public's willingness to support and participate in scientific projects. Data from Experiment suggests an increasing trend in total amounts raised and number of funded projects. As of June 2019, 890 campaigns have been funded from 46,539 contributors, with more than $8 million dollars pledged.

It is demanding to measure the time and effort required for a crowdfunding campaign versus a conventional grant application. It is explicit that any scientist trying to crowdfund a campaign is expected to put in a fair amount of preparation and considerable communication efforts to have a chance of success. But, the advantages and the experience itself can be much more beneficial than a grant application. They might initiate new collaborations, build unexpected links for their research projects, or connect with the public in interesting ways (Vachelard et al., 2016).

A common misunderstanding about science crowdfunding is that only grand campaigns are funded. Almost any topic in science can be appealing to the public. But, it should be clear that campaigns obtaining larger amounts of funding are generally launched by individuals or organizations that have built an audience for their research over a long time. Like other crowdfunding campaigns, public engagement is critical to success in science crowdfunding. Scientist, as creators, should build an audience and actively engage with that audience. Initial audience size and effort in communication can bring in more people to view their campaign pages, leading to successful funding.

As discussed, crowdfunded journalism is journalism that is financially supported by the collection of funding from the public. The potential contributor can judge and support the work of journalists who decide to use crowdfunding as a financial platform. Crowdfunded journalism is a bold movement in the face of giant legacy media, which shapes public opinion. It is effective in promoting public engagement and spreading those important issues.

A group of pioneering journalists have used crowdfunding in a range of ways.[20] Some have raised money to help them cover stories that were underreported or overlooked by mainstream outlets. Others have used crowdfunding for journalism projects that use innovative and interactive storytelling. Established publishers and organizations, both large and small, have used Kickstarter as a lab to innovate, including increased audience engagement and interactivity.

In the Spot.us model, the process of pitching and publishing a campaign for crowdfunded journalism works as follows: A journalist submits a pitch – a short description of the proposed reporting project with a required funding amount. These pitches are then shared with the public on the website with the goal of raising money. Individual contributors can contribute to these stories. When a story on the platform is funded, the journalist may seek an additional venue for publication or publish the stories through their own independent channels. The role of journalism as a storyteller has not changed, but the ways of sharing the story are. People are participating more in the storytelling process.

The membership model, which The Correspondent adopted, works in a different way.[21] They rely on membership fees to fund its journalism, which is slower and more reflective than existing legacy media. Thanks to financial support from their members, they can offer advertisement-free publication. Banning advertisement from the platform helps them stay independent. They do not need to cover less serious topics, such as career and travel. They do not have to compete with huge social media for securing advertising from big clients. Most importantly, they do not have to turn their members into a target for the advertisers. Crowdfunded journalism is not about producing and selling a product but much more about building and growing a community.

For aspiring journalists, especially young and new ones, these new models can be appealing. Crowdfunded journalism might offer them the opportunity to help reinvent news. Most of them want to work without worrying about the demands of an advertiser or the legacy of a giant media brand. New formats can promise audiences coverage that is untainted by scandal or perceived bias. This crowdfunding model also offers a range of experiences. Although those young journalists are not able to participate in the formal training program provided by traditional media outlets, they get daily rotations in addition to editorial jobs. For example, in some membership-based crowdfunding platforms, the tasks could range from researching a topic alongside a more established journalist to help with marketing, membership, and design.

On the contributor side, funding journalism campaigns can make them feel like they are part of a team. They do not pay for a product. They want to join a movement that doesn't depend on the rules of legacy media. Contributors expect crowdfunded news to be a different type of news. It's breaking the power of elite journalism. Ordinary people, by joining this movement, can have a more active, equal part to play in the creation of news. People who support journalism campaigns are not in it for transactions. They join because they want to support something they think is important. They realize crowdfunded journalism is highly dependent on their support. Thus, they also expect that crowdfunded journalism has to answer to their needs instead of those of advertisers.

What researchers found so far

Crowdfunding for social enterprises

A strand of research has focused on the fit between crowdfunding and social enterprises and the significant role of crowdfunding in supporting social enterprises. Our research, with the aggregated survey responses to a campaign level, examined how campaign characteristics influence crowdfunding performance (Ryu and Kim, 2018).[22] We identified societal contributions of campaigns as an important factor determining crowdfunding performance in addition to the other campaign characteristics such as the value of rewards. Although the impact of the reward value is not surprising, the role of societal contribution in drawing more funds indicates a unique aspect of crowdfunding: promoting societal changes. A crowdfunding campaign that proposes values, reward value, and societal contributions to prospective contributors at the same time is more likely to acquire a higher amount of funding. More importantly, successful crowdfunding campaigns with greater societal contributions seem to depend on relatively small amounts of support from a large group of contributors, whereas the greater success of crowdfunding campaigns with higher reward value is mainly due to the financial commitment of a smaller group of highly motivated contributors. The results indicate that a crowdfunding campaign with the potential of contributing to our communities and society for a good reasons may appeal more to larger groups of people, which potentially leads to more collective activities.

Relatedly, Calic and Mosakowski (2016) proposed that creators with a sustainability orientation, possessing goals that concern sustainable gains for individuals and society, such as supporting a community and preserving nature, will experience greater levels of crowdfunding performance than commercial-driven creators. They operationalized sustainability orientation into two dimensions – the social sustainability orientation and the environmental sustainability orientation – by constructing variables representing whether a campaign indicated primarily social or environmental objectives. They tested their propositions with a sample of Kickstarter campaigns in technology and film/video categories and found that sustainability orientation is positively associated to crowdfunding performance for both categories. Those campaigns with either a social or an environmental orientation, compared to (pure) commercial campaigns, recorded higher probability of crowdfunding success and total funding amounts.

Parhankangas and Renko (2017) explored the effect of the linguistic style of a campaign pitch on the performance of the campaigns launched by social enterprises compared to the campaigns of commercial enterprises. They distinguished a social campaign from commercial campaigns by its characteristics that intend to deliver something embedding social benefits. Commercial campaigns refer to projects pursuing to develop new products or services for market. They argued that the expectations for social enterprises and their campaigns are still less established and thus difficult to understand in comparison to the expectations for commercial enterprises in the traditional domains. The expectation for commercial enterprises is much more straightforward and explicit because it can be more easily addressed through different ways, such as the final product and company- and founder-related information. Yet, social enterprises are expected to address ambiguity about expectations through more effective communication approaches and tools for potential contributors. They proposed that social enterprises can obtain this goal by employing appropriate linguistic styles that refine their campaign pitches in more understandable ways for potential contributors and establish an intimate connection to them. They constructed four dimensions of linguistic styles, including concreteness, preciseness, interactivity, and psychological distancing. They examined their propositions with a sample of 656 Kickstarter campaigns, including both social and commercial campaigns, and found that concreteness, preciseness, and interactivity of campaign pitches are positively associated to crowdfunding success for social campaigns, whereas psychological distancing harms the likelihood of success. But, those linguistic styles hardly count for the commercial campaigns.

Crowdfunding for scientific research

Some pioneering studies focused on scientific crowdfunding campaigns. Sauermann et al. (2019) analyzed 725 scientific crowdfunding campaigns on Experiment, the largest platform dedicated to supporting scientific research.

First, descriptive analysis of the sample shows some intriguing facts and figures, including the following:

- A large portion of creators are students: around 30% undergraduate or master students and 25% doctoral students (PhD or MD). Postdocs, assistant professors, and associate or full professors are 7%, 12%, and 17%, respectively.
- Fifty-seven percent of creators are male, and 40% are female. The remaining 3% are organizations.
- Sixty-eight percent of campaigns have single creators, whereas 32% have teams.
- Goal amounts of the campaigns ranged from $100 to more than $100,000. The average goal amount was $6,460 (median value: $3,500).

- The most frequently listed fields are biology, ecology, medicine, engineering, education, psychology, social sciences, and chemistry.
- Around 78% of campaigns aim to conduct scientific investigations of certain topics, whereas 12% aim at the development of things. The other objectives (10%) include protection or restoration of scientific objectives.

Second, they examined the important factors affecting crowdfunding success in the specific context of scientific crowdfunding campaigns. The results indicate that the contributors on the crowdfunding platform may apply different evaluation criteria for those scientific campaigns from the institutional funding agencies for scientific research. For example, the results show that the campaigns launched by students and junior researchers are more likely to achieve goal amounts than those launched by senior scientists. Female scientists enjoy higher success rates over male scientists. Most importantly, previous publication records, considered as important quality information in the domains, are found to have no significant relationship with crowdfunding success.

Finally, interestingly, they explored the factors associated with the press release of crowdfunding campaigns regarding science writers and reporters as a proxy for traditional funding agencies. We can assume that they are more likely to select scientific research based on those traditional evaluation criteria. The results of analysis support this argument. For example, representing relevant previous publications has a strong influence on press coverage, whereas it has no significant effect on crowdfunding success. Similarly, students are less likely to receive press coverage, although they are more likely to obtain the funding successfully than senior scientists. Those differences confirmed the potential role of crowdfunding in supporting important scientific research that may not be of interest from traditional perspectives.

Byrnes et al. (2014) designed a large-scale experiment named #SciFund, a crowdfunding experiment for science, for identifying critical factors influencing scientific crowdfunding campaigns. They coordinated scientists to launch their own crowdfunding campaigns on a crowdfunding platform for their scientific research with the "#SciFund" banner. This experiment ran in rounds, with three rounds in total. Each round, consisting of several months, was divided into three steps: promoting campaign proposals, training contributors, and conducting proposed campaigns. In the first step of each round, the researchers encouraged scientists to engage in crowdfunding practices through different channels such as social media, blogs, and e-mail. A total of 159 scientists participated in the experiment to crowdfund their research. Leveraging data collected from different sources, including participant surveys, campaign-related log data, and social media metrics, they found some important factors affecting campaign success in the context of scientific crowdfunding.

Most of all, comparable to ordinary reward-based crowdfunding, engagement of broader potential contributors is the key to successful scientific crowdfunding. Scientists who plan to launch crowdfunding campaigns for their research are required to build a potential contributor base, hopefully before the launch, via their own social networks. Once the crowdfunding campaigns are launched, they should put effort into managing and cultivating connections between the contributor base and their research through different direct and indirect communication channels. Specifically, reaching out to the contributor base through press coverage could help widen a contributor base and lead them to their crowdfunding campaigns at the same time. Promoting engagement through these communication efforts leads to funds by bringing potential contributors to visit campaign pages.

In the supplementary survey, scientists described some impressions of what is helpful (or not helpful) to promote their crowdfunding campaigns. For the most part, interestingly, the results are remarkably matched to the outcomes of the quantitative analysis described previously. They mentioned friends and family, personal networks, and social media networks as main contributing factors for their success.

In conclusion, potential contributor bases built by promoting efforts result in favorable engagement, finally leading to successful scientific crowdfunding. If any scientists and research institutions plan to tap this new funding source, they are expected to encourage and reward activities that allow them to engage with the crowd.

Crowdfunded journalism

As we discussed in the previous sections, Spot.us played an important role in pioneering crowdfunded journalism. With in-depth interviews of seven journalists who launched their campaigns on Spot.us and eight contributors, Aitamurto (2011) analyzed how crowdfunding potentially affects journalism. The study proposed that crowdfunded journalism demands journalists rethink their roles and responsibilities as journalists to launch to succeed in crowdfunding campaigns. Contributions from readers build strong connections between journalists and contributors. It thus generates another sense of responsibility for the journalist. From the contributors' side, the main motivation is to support social causes and the common good. Individual contributors' motivations are consequently more prosocial and altruistic. Moreover, contributors do not feel a strong sense of connection to the journalists or to the articles to which they contributed. In her following study, for deeper understanding, Aitamurto (2015) examined contributor motivations in supporting crowdfunded journalism. She showed the primary motivations are intrinsic, altruistic, and ideological. By supporting and sharing the campaigns, the contributors want to participate in social change, reduce knowledge asymmetries, empower ordinary people, and generate a more informed public. Learning and deliberation also promote contribution. In the crowdfunded journalism context, contributors basically do not expect monetary rewards like tangible benefits; instead, they hope to join building a better community, and crowdfunded journalism becomes a channel for social change. Relatedly, Jian and Shin (2015) identified motivations behind contributors at Spot.us based on self-reported survey data from 344 respondents and those respondents' transaction records obtained from the database.[23] They explored nine different motivations, including altruism, fun, belief in freedom of content, social, community, self-esteem, understanding, image, and family and friends. Among those nine motivations, belief in freedom of content, altruism, and community were highly valued by contributors according to the survey results, whereas fun and family and friends are positive influencers for actual contribution level.

Hunter (2016), based on in-depth interviews with 27 journalists who launched their crowdfunding campaigns on different crowdfunding platforms, including Kickstarter, Indiegogo, and Spot.us, explored potential roles of crowdfunding in journalism and how journalists prospect the roles. Most of all, those journalists found crowdfunding is an extremely labor-intensive practice as design and promotion of the campaigns require great amounts of time and resources. The practice of asking for money from the public is uncomfortable for most journalists as preaching their idea to the public is not comparable to norms and routines that they are familiar with. Yet, some of them are quite open to become more transparent about their work by considering it a part of the change to involve audiences more in creating news. Moreover, they feel empowerment by being able to create news outside of legacy media. It provides journalists with a sense that they have the power to change how journalism works, even at a small scale. Most of them adopt crowdfunding because they want to share stories that they expect not to be reported in legacy media. Many journalists appreciate the freedom crowdfunding offers them in this regard.

Most journalists participating in the interviews mentioned that they did not collect a lot of funding from their campaigns. But, they think that crowdfunding will initiate new opportunities for them. For example, journalists who are beginning their careers, and more experienced freelancers, hope that crowdfunding will allow them to either kick-start a job as a journalist or pursue the profession as a freelancer. Moreover, it provides a place where new experimental journalism can obtain initial funding, leveraging it to further expand audience reach.

Jian and Usher (2014), focusing on individual contributors' monetary support for crowdfunded news, analyzed 210 campaigns and contributors of those campaigns on Spot.us. Regarding the content of campaigns, the results show that contributors were more interested in news related to immediate concerns for them – public health and city infrastructure – than more critical news about their community, such as government, politics, and media accountability. The results are somewhat surprising because contributors were expected to be more interested in community-related news surveilling important facts than guidance for daily living as they were participating in an experiment on a new type of journalism for serving their community better. Yet, this result does not mitigate value of crowdfunded journalism as it suggests an opportunity for audiences to express their interests and preferences for news content. Interestingly, opposed to the expectation again, they also found that less experienced journalists are more favored by contributors than their experienced counterparts. Then, why might less experienced journalists perform better in crowdfunded journalism? They suggested it may reflect how much effort journalists put in their crowdfunding

98 *Beauty of crowdfunding*

campaigns. Experienced journalists may have access to other financing sources, making them less dependent on crowdfunding and thus investing less effort into their campaigns.

A new hope: civic crowdfunding

In 2014, the London City Hall started a new experiment to explore how it could initiate a new way of turning local knowledge and ideas into reality.[24] Grassroots groups of citizens can propose campaign ideas directly to City Hall and gain access to funding and support to realize them. This project has to date been administered using a UK-based crowdfunding platform, Spacehive, where public campaigns are used to share ideas and establish local support, promoting community engagement. City Hall has pledged more than £1.7 million to 103 crowdfunding campaigns across the capital since 2014. These were run by people just like us. Nearly 14,000 Londoners have come together to raise an extra £2.8 million in pledges toward these campaigns. They include a study to turn an old rail track into a city garden, a community grocery store, and a market to help unemployed people find work and a community-led museum and training kitchen. For example, a social enterprise set up by three citizens who work in design, retail, and architecture proposed to transform a dilapidated overpass in Liverpool into an urban walkway and park that cost less than its proposed demolition.[25] They ran a campaign on Spacehive in 2014 and gained support. They raised £43,809 for the full feasibility study, and they have been working in partnership with the city council to move to the next steps.

All these campaigns show innovation and enterprise. The program gives people more input and control over the way London develops. They demonstrate active citizenship with an aspiration for wider social good. Every year, City Hall pledges up to 75% of the total project cost (up to £50,000) to the best ideas. The mayor, as a representative of City Hall, pledges the funds across campaigns, catalyzing a 95% success rate. Over the last rounds, the crowd has pledged £1.80 for every £1 pledged by City Hall.

As we found from this example, with the crowdfunding model, a more straightforward approach for improving communities and society recently has arisen: civic crowdfunding, a crowdfunding practice for providing services to communities and society (Davies, 2015). Civic crowdfunding campaigns represent a less transactional, consumerist interaction than many projects observed on Kickstarter and Indiegogo, in which contributors mainly look to obtain rewards. Campaigns launched through civic crowdfunding are diverse, with outputs including community gathering places, transportation options, and assorted public services. Many events have been crowdfunded; however, infrastructure projects also represent a significant proportion of successfully funded civic projects. Civic crowdfunding suits local contributors and a geographically proximate community, that is, those who can make use of, and benefit from, the crowdfunded campaigns. In the case of civic crowdfunding, where the reward is access to the completed local project, self-interest is not just individual but also a collective and self-and-others-interest.

Basically, thus, none of the civic crowdfunding platforms are global (i.e., creators and contributors are all from within the country of platform origin), which lends itself to a more local support base than Kickstarter or Indiegogo, with campaigns and funders from around the world.

Civic crowdfunding is still an emerging field. Few large projects have been funded and completed. Nevertheless, it already represents a concrete opportunity to create links between and among communities as well as new joint efforts between residents and subnational governments to promote sustainable and inclusive local development. As expected, creators of civic crowdfunding campaigns are often municipalities and organizations, and funding frequently follows a tripod model, with financial support from across three parties, including a government body, for-profit or not-for-profit business or organization, and individual contributors. But, individual creators are able to initiate a campaign for leveraging this tripod model. If campaign creators convince contributors to finance a particular project, they may target specific areas that remain inaccessible to inhabitants from other areas. Civic crowdfunded campaigns can specially aim to address some territorial inequalities by providing access to a specific local public good to residents from distressed areas.

Although civic crowdfunding's potential is underdeveloped, there is an upward trend in the number of campaigns in both crowdfunding platforms. For example, Kickstarter has also hosted some civic crowdfunding campaigns, such as the LowLine, a campaign aiming to turn an abandoned underground terminal in New York into a public park.[26] Up to 3,300 contributors participated in the campaign with $155,186. Indiegogo has also launched several campaigns under its community category, conforming to a definition of civic crowdfunding. As of June 2019, Spacehive has funded £13 million from 650 campaigns since going live in 2012.[27] US-based Ioby has successfully funded more than 2,000 civic crowdfunding campaigns and raised $6 million since its launch in 2009.[28]

Some pioneering studies have been done on civic crowdfunding to date that provide quantitative and qualitative empirical evidence. Davies (2014) analyzed 1,224 civic crowdfunding campaigns collected between June 2012 and March 2014, of which 771 were successful. These campaigns come from seven different platforms hosting civic crowdfunding campaigns, both civic and generic platforms located in four different countries.[29] The data set shows that the average individual pledge across campaigns was around $204,[30] and the average amount raised by completed projects was $9,502. Civic crowdfunding campaigns mostly tackle neighborhood issues such as a project launching small size parks in a city that provides a public benefit for an underserved area. Stiver et al. (2015) emphasized the role of community in civic crowdfunding because community propels campaign activity. In the context of civic crowdfunding, both online and offline communities are central to civic crowdfunding. Transitions between online and off-line community are a distinguishing feature of civic crowdfunding, with citizens rallying around projects online as well as mobilizing for participation off-line. Given the public good nature of civic crowdfunding, Hassna et al. (2018) focus on the influence that institutional lead contributors have on subsequent fundraising outcomes and how that influence varies depending on the organization type, including businesses, government entities, and nongovernmental organizations (NGOs). Analyzing data from Spacehive, they showed that securing lead contributions from established organizations of any type is significantly associated with subsequent campaign fundraising success, and those lead contributions are particularly beneficial when supported by NGOs. They also found that lead donations operate by increasing average pledge amounts rather than the number of individuals offering pledges. The results suggest that attracting lead contributions may not be a particularly effective mechanism for building awareness but for providing more credibility to those who are more likely to participate in the campaigns.

In conclusion, civic crowdfunding represents not only an opportunity to secure funds and complete projects but also a way to forge partnerships across government bodies, businesses, and citizens and to foster the development of local communities. The current diversity of campaigns suggests that civic crowdfunding has the potential to develop in multiple ways to satisfy various needs. We have also advocated for careful consideration of the role of online platforms alongside off-line efforts. Future iterations of civic crowdfunding might work effectively, united with off-line efforts, integrating online tools and off-line funding approaches.

Key takeaways

- Crowdfunding has the potential to change the world to a better place by tapping vital but neglected domains, such as social enterprises, scientific research, and journalism.
- Crowdfunding has emerged to address the different needs of social enterprises. As crowdfunding combines social values, social networks, and alternative reward systems, it responds to the financial and communal needs of social enterprises. Crowdfunding and social enterprises are a good match as contributors in the crowdfunding context generally look at the ideas and core values of the campaign rather than expected returns.
- Scientists are also increasingly considering crowdfunding to support their research. The power of science crowdfunding goes beyond financial rewards as it has the potential to connect science and society in a better way. It is a promising alternative, particularly for researchers at the beginning of their careers who are unable to compete for grants with renowned scientists.
- Journalists have used crowdfunding in different ways as it is effective to promote public engagement and spread important issues. Crowdfunded journalism is a bold movement in the face of giant legacy media, which shapes public opinion, as it helps cover stories that are underreported or overlooked by the legacy media.
- Civic crowdfunding, a crowdfunding practice for providing services to communities and society, is emerging as a way to change the world into a better place. It suits local contributors and a geographically proximate community as the reward is access to the completed local project. Civic crowdfunding

campaigns also aim to address territorial inequalities by providing access to a needed local public facility to residents.

Notes

1. www.indiegogo.com/projects/who-gives-a-crap-toilet-paper-that-builds-toilets
2. https://us.whogivesacrap.org
3. www.fastcoexist.com/1679719/build-your-own-civilization-with-the-global-village-construction-set
4. www.kickstarter.com/projects/622508883/global-village-construction-set
5. www.opensourceecology.org/gvcs/
6. www.fastcompany.com/3027882/social-entrepreneurs-dont-forget-about-kickstarter
7. https://experiment.com/projects/how-does-natural-gas-fracking-contribute-to-air-pollution
8. www.sciencemag.org/news/2018/03/want-crowdfund-your-science-new-study-hints-who-successful
9. https://experiment.com/projects/finding-a-cure-for-batten-disease
10. www.journalism.co.uk/news/long-form-digital-journalism-site-matter-launches/s2/a551191/
11. www.kickstarter.com/projects/readmatter/matter
12. http://mediashift.org/2015/03/why-crowdfunded-journalism-pioneer-spot-us-died/
13. https://decorrespondent.nl
14. www.nbcnews.com/news/all/dutch-news-startup-has-crowdfunded-1-million-unbreak-u-s-n943266
15. www.cjr.org/the_media_today/crowdfunding-correspondent-office.php
16. https://thecorrespondent.com
17. According to its website, it would start publishing on 30 September 2019.
18. www.fastcompany.com/3027882/social-entrepreneurs-dont-forget-about-kickstarter
19. www.forbes.com/sites/devinthorpe/2018/04/30/8-keys-to-crowdfunding-success-for-social-entrepreneurs/
20. https://ijnet.org/en/story/kickstarter-hopes-improve-odds-crowdfunded-journalism-projects
21. https://medium.com/de-correspondent/a-short-guide-to-crowdfunding-journalism-b495ecba710
22. We aggregated the contributor-level data to campaign-level characteristic scales by calculating the average values of individual contributor responses for a focal campaign. For the analysis, we used a validated project-level data set of 100 campaigns from the 366 contributor responses.
23. Spot.us also contributed to the literature by providing a rich data set for researchers who studied this topic. It tracked all the detailed records on most transactions and activities on the website, such as characteristics of the campaigns, creator (i.e., journalist) information, funding amounts, and characteristics of individual contributors.
24. www.london.gov.uk/what-we-do/regeneration/funding-opportunities/crowdfund-london
25. www.spacehive.com/theflyoverliverpool
26. www.kickstarter.com/projects/855802805/lowline-an-underground-park-on-nycs-lower-east-sid
27. www.spacehive.com/about
28. www.ioby.org/about

29 Catarse (Brazil), Goteo (Spain), Spacehive (UK), Ioby, Neighborly, Kickstarter, and Citizinvestor (US).
30 The average amount is relatively larger compared to the ordinary crowdfunding context because the civic crowdfunding campaigns may include institutional contributors, such as municipalities and government entities.

References

Aitamurto, T. 2011. The Impact of Crowdfunding on Journalism: Case Study of Spot: Us, a Platform for Community-Funded Reporting. *Journalism Practice*, 5, 429–445.

Aitamurto, T. 2015. Motivation Factors in Crowdsourced Journalism: Social Impact, Social Change, and Peer Learning. *International Journal of Communication*, 9, 3523–3543.

Byrnes, J. E., Ranganathan, J., Walker, B. L. & Faulkes, Z. 2014. To Crowdfund Research, Scientists Must Build an Audience for Their Work. *PLoS One*, 9, e110329.

Calic, G. & Mosakowski, E. 2016. Kicking Off Social Entrepreneurship: How A Sustainability Orientation Influences Crowdfunding Success. *Journal of Management Studies*, 53, 738–767.

Davies, R. 2014. Civic Crowdfunding as a Marketplace for Participation in Urban Development. *Proceedings of the Internet, Policy & Politics Conference 2014*, Oxford, United Kingdom.

Davies, R. 2015. Three Provocations for Civic Crowdfunding. *Information, Communication & Society*, 18, 342–355.

Hassna, G., Burtch, G., Lee, C. H. & Zhao, J. L. 2018. Understanding the Role of Lead Donor Types in Civic Crowdfunding. *Social Science Research Network*. Available at: https://ssrn.com/abstract=3175916.

Hunter, A. 2016. "It's Like Having a Second Full-Time Job" Crowdfunding, Journalism and Labour. *Journalism Practice*, 10, 217–232.

Jian, L. & Shin, J. 2015. Motivations Behind Donors' Contributions to Crowdfunded Journalism. *Mass Communication and Society*, 18, 165–185.

Jian, L. & Usher, N. 2014. Crowd-Funded Journalism. *Journal of Computer-Mediated Communication*, 19, 155–170.

Lehner, O. M. 2013. Crowdfunding Social Ventures: A Model and Research Agenda. *Venture Capital*, 15, 289–311.

Parhankangas, A. & Renko, M. 2017. Linguistic Style and Crowdfunding Success Among Social and Commercial Entrepreneurs. *Journal of Business Venturing*, 32, 215–236.

Ryu, S. & Kim, Y-G. 2018. Money Is Not Everything: A Typology of Crowdfunding Project Creators. *Journal of Strategic Information Systems*, 27, 350–368.

Sauermann, H., Franzoni, C. & Shafi, K. 2019. Crowdfunding Scientific Research: Descriptive Insights and Correlates of Funding Success. *PLoS One*, 14, e0208384.

Stiver, A., Barroca, L., Minocha, S., Richards, M. & Roberts, D. 2015. Civic Crowdfunding Research: Challenges, Opportunities, and Future Agenda. *New Media & Society*, 17, 249–271.

Vachelard, J., Gambarra-Soares, T., Augustini, G., Riul, P. & Maracaja-Coutinho, V. 2016. A Guide to Scientific Crowdfunding. *PLoS Biology*, 14, e1002373.

Wheat, R. E., Wang, Y., Byrnes, J. E. & Ranganathan, J. 2013. Raising Money for Scientific Research Through Crowdfunding. *Trends in Ecology & Evolution*, 28, 71–72.

Part 3
Behind crowdfunding

10 Key challenges and drawbacks of crowdfunding

Crowdfunding is not an easy task, as many creators assume. The first chapter of this part presents some key challenges and potential drawbacks of crowdfunding: Fulfillment of the contributors, potential risk of fraud, and protection of ideas are representative examples of those in crowdfunding practices. This chapter also offers possible resolutions for those challenges and drawbacks.

Some big disasters in crowdfunding history

With more than $13 million raised from 62,642 contributors in August 2014, the Coolest Cooler (the Coolest, hereafter) remains one of the most successful campaigns in crowdfunding history.[1] The Coolest can store 55 quarts of beverages, and was featured with some functions such as a Bluetooth speaker, cocktail blender, and bottle opener. When Ryan Grepper, founder and CEO of the company, launched the Kickstarter campaign for the Coolest, he planned to deliver the product to contributors in February 2015. But, the unexpectedly huge success of the campaign significantly increased demand, complexity of production, and shipping. Being made in China, due to the change in scale, all the processes for production and shipping took longer than expected. In February 2015, the company announced a delay of delivery to July 2015, noting that upgrades of some features were partial reasons for the postponement.

The contributors, however, found that the company was selling the Coolest on Amazon, frustrating them.[2] In a video uploaded to their YouTube channel, Grepper said that the Amazon sale was to raise enough money to continue producing new batches of units for contributors. The contributors were definitely not happy. One-star reviews for the Coolest on Amazon were flooding in from those angry contributors, asking why the products had not been delivered to them first.

The problem was in its blending motor. Its supplier was on strike at production time, but the Coolest could not find a viable replacement. The company announced another delay after testing another blending motor from an alternative supplier as it could not meet the company's required standards. Even if a new motor had passed the company's quality testing process, it would have taken up to a month for a supplier to produce enough of them for the required volume. High shipping costs also caused problems. The company brought the large box containing every Coolest to the company's headquarters to Portland, Oregon, from which they were then exported all around the world.

The company finally began shipping in July 2015 and sent out tens of thousands of units until the end of that year. But, that was all. In March 2016, the company admitted that production had stopped, and it was seeking additional investments, with a part of this to be used for fulfilling the rewards toward the remaining contributors.[3] In April 2016, it added an option to pay an extra $97 for expedited shipping for those still waiting for the promised reward.[4] The company emphasized the option as a sort of benefit as the total price was still below the regular retail price for the product. It also indicated that the idea came from contributors. In May 2016, it was reported that around 10,000 contributors had picked up this option, and production resumed. In addition to this, it announced that the company was preparing to seek additional funding for the Coolest via CircleUp, an equity-based crowdfunding platform.[5]

In September 2016, after receiving 315 consumer complaints during the fulfillment phase, the Oregon Department of Justice (DOJ) confirmed that it was investigating the company.[6] In June 2017, the company entered into an agreement with the Oregon DOJ, stating that the plan for fulfilling the remaining rewards for contributors was in a three-year time frame. With the agreement, the company announced that the Coolest was unlikely to be seen soon as the company needed to make money before it could make more products.[7] Grepper said the only way to fulfill the rewards for those remaining contributors was to sell more products in retail channels and thus make more money. It was frustrating for those who first pledged to the company in 2014, thinking they should receive their products first.

The contributors to Coolest were not the most severe victims of a crowdfunding problem. In December 2015, Kickstarter hired Mark Harris, an investigative journalist in the tech domain, to figure out and report on the Zano mini-drone, one of the platform's most high-profile campaigns that failed to fulfill the promised rewards.

The Zano successfully raised more than £2.3 million ($3.5 million) and was the most-funded Kickstarter campaign in Europe.[8] But Torquing Group, the UK-based drone venture driving the campaign, totally fell apart in less than a year after the campaign. Most of the 12,000 contributors, who had pledged their money and ended up with nothing in their hands, poured blame on the platform, Kickstarter, in addition to having angry words for the company. When Torquing Group announced that it was closing its business, Kickstarter insisted on its disorientation over the disaster and commissioned Mark Harris to investigate what happened during and after the campaign.

Mark Harris flew to South Wales and spent six weeks collecting the facts from as many people as he could reach so that he could produce an accountable report of the Zano case.[9] In his report, with more than 13,000 words, he explained the origins of the Zano. The business was basically based on the personal goals of its founder Ivan Reedman, a self-taught engineer, to build a commercial drone. The passionate team, despite lacking expertise and experience, turned the Zano into a crowdfunding campaign and made a big hit, overwhelmingly surpassing its original monetary goal. After this sensational success, disaster awaited as Reedman and his team realized they did not have the expertise and experience to manage the situation and fulfill the rewards they promised.[10]

Fulfillment of crowdfunding campaigns: a demanding but manageable task

The Coolest and the Zano are not alone. According to a survey on Kickstarter creators, among successfully funded campaigns across the domains, a failure to fulfill the rewards accounts for around 9% of all campaigns.[11] Even cultural and arts campaigns, of course, fall through.[12] In 2009, for example, musician Josh Dibb raised $26,000 for traveling to Mali and recording an album there. Even now, his contributors still cannot enjoy a single limited-edition-LP chord that he promised them. As we can assume, fulfillment of the crowdfunding campaigns is demanding for all the genres and categories. But, the issue is specifically critical with hardware.

In hardware campaigns, around 80% of the creators deliver their rewards to the contributors with considerable delays.[13] Most of them do finally ship something, but about 14% of the campaigns in the analysis have delivered either nothing at all or something with much lower quality than promised. Many campaigns were delayed or failed for a variety of reasons. Some cases went over budget for additional features. In addition, creators are expected to package the rewards, figure out appropriate shipping options, and pray that they arrive on time without any issues.

Creators seeking to crowdfund their projects should account for potential, mostly existing, challenges in managing the whole process in addition to pure development and production efforts. The job of handling a long list of contributors, shipping the rewards, and communicating with contributors is demanding and time-consuming. When a large number of contributors participate in a campaign, creators will face even greater administrative challenges.

For addressing the issue, an entire new domain is emerging to help crowdfunding creators. Platform operators fully promote knowledge sharing among the creators in fulfillment of the campaigns. For example, Kickstarter launched a new section of its platform, named Campus, where creators can share and discuss advice and concerns.[14] Indiegogo teamed up with Arrow Electronics, a consumer electronics device company, to help creators deliver rewards with engineering support and assistance in building a go-to-market strategy.[15] Some independent players provide outsourcing service for creators.[16] They act as partners to help fulfillment of the campaign. They are in charge of all the administrative works required for preparing the promised rewards on time. If some campaigns are not large enough to commission those fulfillment partners, those creators, and the other creators as well, can follow the advice that follows:[17,18,19]

- Set up a realistic, detailed plan with preparation for scaling up: Do not underestimate the difference between a prototype and real production. Especially important, put considerable focus on operation management and supply chain. Any updates in design or packaging may cause rebooting of the whole production process. That could likely take additional time and uncounted resources. Moreover, as all the preparations change at different scales, it is therefore expected to sometime reinitiate the entire plan for production and delivery. Some can make a hundred products in a garage but cannot make several thousand. Each scale level requires its own costs and resources. Every creator is expected to conduct considerable research on a number of manufacturers and other partners and set up a detailed Plan B, and C, if possible.
- Compromise properly among quality, budget, and timeline: For all of the creators, the final goal would be to deliver a significant reward to their contributors as planned. But, they come to realize, when the campaign is closed, the goal was not realistic at all. In most cases, creators are in a situation in which they are expected to choose one or two priorities in quality of the reward, budget for production and delivery, and/or timeline. Although the most optimal solution is to deliver a reward with the promised quality on time within budget, it hardly happens in the real situation. Mostly, creators would choose the case of delivering a high-quality reward within budget, but with a delayed timeline as they cannot give up the quality or expand the budget dramatically. But, for various reasons, creators should compromise the trade-off, especially between quality and timeline. A moderate delay could be accepted among the contributors, but the degree of expectation and satisfaction or dissatisfaction sometimes rely on the timing of delivery. Even though there is a promising opportunity to improve the quality of the reward by adding a new feature or function, if it takes much more cost and resources than expected, creators should leave the option for future development. Most importantly, for managing any unexpected delays in the fulfillment process, close and transparent communication with contributors is key.
- Engage in close and transparent communication with contributors: After each campaign, every creator has a group of supporters to keep in the community. For those supporters, during the fulfillment process, creators need to keep them informed with every step of the process. They deserve their questions being answered and their concerns being resolved. Even though creators cannot avoid some angry words in the case of unexpected delay, close communication and transparency will mitigate the situation. Make sure that crowdfunded money is not the final goal of crowdfunding. It is a part of how crowdfunding can support the creators. Through the fulfillment process, creators are building a business and a community, not a product itself. Some important things always take longer than what we expect them to take.

Potential risks: how to protect crowdfunders and a crowdfunded idea

From another perspective, related to the fulfillment of rewards, crowdfunding is not free from the concern of fraud (Valanciene and Jegeleviciute, 2013). As there are only loose requirements for posting a crowdfunding campaign in most crowdfunding platforms, it can become a precondition for fraud via crowdfunding in various ways. Due to the reduced requirements for public disclosure, some creators can try to hide true information. Also, some campaigns might even be launched as a fraud. Some can launch a campaign articulated with fake information to receive funding and spend it all for different purposes. More importantly, some crowdfunding contributors in crowdfunding lack expertise in evaluating feasibility and run the risk of losing money to fraud. The online setting for crowdfunding also makes it more difficult for contributors to evaluate whether a crowdfunding campaign is reliable or not. For example, some crowdfunding platforms out to raise money for different causes, including local cultural projects and medical expenses, have been criticized for not providing enough controls to protect contributors from potential fraud as the platforms are operated as for-profit entities.[20] Those platforms tend to focus more on increasing the number of campaigns launched, but efforts to check accountability of each crowdfunding campaign are not sufficient.

In the crowdfunding context, creators mainly rely on voluntary disclosure to showcase their capabilities and campaign quality. But, without the lack of clear regulations or guidelines, there has been no trustworthy mechanism (e.g., auditing by an independent third party) for certifying the information posted by the creators. Moreover, the event-like nature of most campaigns (many creators launch their campaigns only once) may make the disclosure less credible.

Despite its shortcomings, however, crowdfunding platforms seem to be considerably fraud resistant (Mollick, 2014). Most of all, due to its open nature, every campaign is under examination from different potential contributors. Although an individual contributor lacks expertise in detecting fraud, the "wisdom of crowds" works properly for filtering out fraud and unqualified campaigns in the crowdfunding context. Addressing the issue, many crowdfunding platforms started to regulate creators to disclose any potential risks related to their campaigns. Some also note whether the creators possess the ability to deal with the risks in the campaign description. For example, beginning in September 2012, Kickstarter requests that all new campaigns prepare a risks and challenges section in their campaign descriptions.[21] In September 2014, Kickstarter again announced that it would change its terms of use to strengthen the contractual position of contributors by clarifying the nature of the contract between creators and contributors.[22] With this change, Kickstarter aimed at preventing potential hazards from creators by clearly indicating creators' obligations to fulfill the promised rewards (or refund pledged amounts in case of failure), including the possibility of legal action against creators.

Those actions seem to work properly in some respect. A study showed that more disclosure of risks and challenges has a positive relationship with probability of a campaign being successfully funded and total funding amounts.[23] It suggests that contributors value the disclosure by creators when making a decision to pledge funding for a crowdfunding campaign.

Another risk from the other side is that creators seeking to crowdfund for their campaigns face the chance of their idea being stolen. There are numerous potential competitors and large corporations in the same domains. Creators might lack knowledge about how to protect their ideas. Moreover, if the idea is taken, most creators lack the resources to manage the situation. This fear of disclosure is quite intuitive as other players could easily imitate the idea once they realized its advantages and potential. Creators may also feel concern about the disclosure of information with strategic value, such as launch timing and product price.

Although the potential role of crowdfunding platforms might be reactive and limited in protecting the intellectual property of any crowdfunded ideas, creators could take action to prevent the worst scenario.[24] Most of all, creators are expected to choose crowdfunding platforms carefully according to how different platforms force information disclosure in the campaign description. Creators should also have a clear and concrete plan for coming up with potential infringement related to their product offering before disclosing campaign information publicly. Depending on the campaign and product types, creators may restrict the critical information related to core intellectual property as confidential content. If there is no explicit way to develop a protection strategy, creators may choose to delay its disclosure as long as they can. Use of the update feature in many crowdfunding platforms could be an alternative. Relatedly, creators should nail down a plan for product offering before posting information publicly, not only for protecting ideas but also for fulfilling the promised rewards. Creators should be aware that there is potential for leakage when launching a crowdfunding campaign. With this explicit risk, however, creators can enjoy many benefits outweighing the costs by leveraging contributors to reach out for help.

Dark side of crowdfunding

In the Part 2, we discussed many benefits of crowdfunding in addressing several important issues. As part of the platform economy, crowdfunding leverages the crowd to provide different values, such as funding, information, or community. Some people may wonder if crowdfunding only has only a bright side. No, it also has its own dark side, which limits the potential of crowdfunding to perform as a change maker.[25]

For example, a considerable portion of crowdfunding campaigns have become an excuse to leave more basic public services up to the crowd.[26] Some platforms allow people to turn to crowdfunding for many different purposes in addition to creative ideas. Paying for funerals, subsidizing medical expenses, and supporting maternity leave are examples.[27] The scope of these campaigns are limited at this moment, but their use is expanding considerably. If crowdfunding is used for privatizing what was once – or should be – supported by the public sector, some government agencies may push for those expenses to be covered by the crowd. The effect could weaken the competitiveness of crowdfunding in promoting creativity and innovation.

Even in the creative and cultural sectors, some drawbacks exist.[28] One aspect is that crowdfunding's advantages may not be equally distributed across the different genres and types of campaigns. For example, campaigns providing tangible, pre-ordered products, such as DVDs and tickets, are more likely to succeed in crowdfunding compared to those that need longer-term support and provide intangible, abstract outcomes, such as new skills. Campaigns that offer more personal experiences, such as dance and painting, are less likely to reach the crowd in the online setting, whereas other genres are more suitable to be experienced and delivered online. It indicates that crowdfunding may be more suitable for certain types of cultural and creative domains.

Moreover, crowdfunding tends to reinforce existing inequalities in some senses. Reputation built in the conventional setting could be amplified on crowdfunding platforms, confirming the "money makes more money" mantra. There is no doubt that any existing positive reputation leads to more successful crowdfunding campaigns. Actually, there is a considerable number of campaigns launched by established corporations and famous figures in some cultural and creative domains. Some of these outperform the "ordinary" campaigns, even though their main purpose is not raising money itself. Those established players' participation may limit the full potential of crowdfunding to democratize the capital market, but it also has a positive effect on drawing attention from wider ranges of the crowd, and this expands the whole industry.

Key takeaways

- In addition to pure development and production efforts, creators should account for potential challenges in managing the whole process in fulfillment of rewards. Especially, when a large number of contributors participate in a campaign, creators will face even greater administrative challenges. For addressing the challenge, creators are expected to set up a realistic, detailed plan; compromise among quality, budget, and timeline; and communicate closely with contributors.
- Despite the concern for fraud, crowdfunding platforms seem to be considerably fraud resistant. In the crowdfunding context, the "wisdom of crowds" works properly for filtering out fraud and unqualified campaigns. Addressing the risk, crowdfunding platforms regulate creators to disclose any potential risks related to their campaigns and how to deal with them.
- Creators face the risk of their ideas being stolen due to its open nature. Although the potential role of crowdfunding platforms might be reactive and limited in protecting the intellectual property of any crowdfunded ideas, creators could take action to prevent the worst-case scenario.

- Undoubtedly, crowdfunding has its own dark side, which limits its potential as a change maker. A considerable portion of crowdfunding campaigns may become an excuse to leave more basic public services up to the crowd. Even in the creative sectors, crowdfunding's advantages may not equally benefit different types of campaigns. Crowdfunding also tends to reinforce existing inequalities as reputations built in conventional settings could be amplified on crowdfunding platforms.

Notes

1. www.kickstarter.com/projects/ryangrepper/coolest-cooler-21st-century-cooler-thats-actually
2. www.theverge.com/2015/11/18/9758214/coolest-cooler-amazon-kickstater-shipping-production-delay
3. www.theverge.com/2016/4/13/11424924/coolest-cooler-kickstarter-disaster-delays
4. www.theverge.com/2016/4/13/11424924/coolest-cooler-kickstarter-disaster-delays
5. www.crowdfundinsider.com/2016/03/82461-coolest-cooler-will-raise-additional-capital-via-equity-crowdfunding/
6. https://consumerist.com/2016/09/30/oregon-department-of-justice-announces-investigation-against-coolest/
7. www.geekwire.com/2017/thousands-kickstarter-backers-still-waiting-coolest-cooler-may-wait-another-3-years/
8. www.vice.com/en_us/article/ezp434/kickstarter-is-funding-investigative-journalism-about-a-failed-kickstarter
9. www.bbc.com/news/technology-35356147
10. https://medium.com/@meharris/how-zano-raised-millions-on-kickstarter-and-left-backers-with-nearly-nothing-85c0abe4a6cb#.boybm1jh4
11. www.kickstarter.com/fulfillment
12. www.nytimes.com/2015/05/03/magazine/zpm-espresso-and-the-rage-of-the-jilted-crowdfunder.html
13. www.kickstarter.com/fulfillment
14. www.kickstarter.com/blog/welcome-to-campus
15. http://techcrunch.com/2016/05/20/indiegogo-teams-up-with-arrow/
16. www.crowdcrux.com/top-kickstarter-fulfillment-companies/
17. https://techcrunch.com/2014/10/11/8-things-about-hardware-crowdfunding-we-learned-from-20-campaigns/
18. https://tech.co/news/crowdfunding-hardware-fails-often-2017-10
19. www.theverge.com/2016/4/19/11461278/crowdfunding-hardware-flic-memory
20. www.wsj.com/articles/crowdfunding-sites-like-gofundme-and-youcaring-raise-moneyand-concerns-1456775949
21. www.theverge.com/2012/9/20/3365880/kickstarter-new-project-guidelines-risks-challenges
22. www.kickstarter.com/blog/an-update-to-our-terms-of-use
23. https://blogs.lse.ac.uk/businessreview/2019/05/15/disclosure-helps-project-creators-get-crowdfunding-on-kickstarter/
24. www.inc.com/christina-desmarais/how-to-protect-your-intellectual-property-when-crowdfunding-5-tips.html
25. www.arts.gov/national-initiatives/creativity-connects/report/how-does-crowdfunding-change-the-picture-for-artists

26 www.wired.com/2016/03/crowdfunding-is-evil
27 www.washingtonpost.com/news/parenting/wp/2016/04/16/why-desperate-mothers-are-turning-to-crowdfunding-to-pay-for-maternity-leave/
28 www.arts.gov/national-initiatives/creativity-connects/report/how-does-crowdfunding-change-the-picture-for-artists

References

Mollick, E. 2014. The Dynamics of Crowdfunding: An Exploratory Study. *Journal of Business Venturing*, 29, 1–16.

Valanciene, L. & Jegeleviciute, S. 2013. Valuation of Crowdfunding: Benefits and Drawbacks. *Economics and Management*, 18, 39–48.

11 What comes next after crowdfunding

They lived happily ever after? Subsequent benefits of crowdfunding success

What happens after crowdfunding? Many stakeholders, including creators and researchers, have extensively focused on the factors that determine campaign success on crowdfunding platforms, but emphasis on what happens after a crowdfunding campaign is relatively sparse. There are many opportunities to expand our understanding of the consequences of crowdfunding for different venture outcomes.

We have learned what could happen after successful crowdfunding campaigns from some cases.

- Oculus, we discussed many times in some of the chapters, received a round of VC investment after the success of their crowdfunding campaign and was later acquired by Facebook for $2 billion.
- PyroPet started with a cat candle called Kisa. Once the carved candle melts down, a gorgeous metal skeleton is revealed. It launched a Kickstarter campaign in 2013 and raised more than double its $40,000 goal.[1] Through the campaign, PyroPet drew attention from potential core customers and the press. It now sells lots of different animal-shaped candles in some mainstream channels, including Amazon.[2]
- Scanadu Scout, a device that measures vital signs of a person and forwards the information to a connected mobile application, raised about $1.7 million on Indiegogo in 2013.[3] After the crowdfunding, it raised a series of follow-up investments, around $49.7 million in total, from multiple investors until the end of 2015. But, in 2016, it closed down all the related product lines it had provided as it failed to obtain approval from the Food and Drug Administration for use of the products in a medical context.

In addition to fundraising for the campaigns, crowdfunding provides additional advantages. That include feedback and suggestions from contributors, acquisition of an initial group of loyal customers, and follow-up fundraising opportunities. A survey of the creators who attempted to raise money on Kickstarter suggested that crowdfunding offered many benefits beyond the funding itself. It helps creators acquire access to users, media, and employees.[4] According to the survey, since the Kickstarter campaigns, creators added an average of 2.2 new employees per successful campaign. Regarding the follow-up financing outcomes, another study conducted in 2014 argued that 9.5% of hardware ventures crowdfunded on Kickstarter or Indiegogo obtained VC investments.[5]

Of course, this doesn't mean that those crowdfunded ventures won't fail in the end as you can see the case of Scanadu Scout. But, there is no doubt that crowdfunded ventures enjoy some benefits after a successful campaign, and their development differs from non-crowdfunded ventures or ventures that obtained financing via other sources.

We expect three different types of subsequent benefits of crowdfunding success. First, crowdfunding success generates some operational advantage. Actually, more than 90% of successful design, technology, and video game campaigns on Kickstarter appear to remain ongoing ventures one to four years after their campaigns.[6] The crowdfunding success helps organizations find and recruit employees as it proves the competitiveness and attractiveness of the organizations. It also generates a positive effect in securing business partnerships for the same reason.

Second, it offers another advantage for marketing purposes. Due to its open nature, crowdfunding helps bring attention from important stakeholders to the campaigns. The press is one group. Especially for those who have raised larger amounts of funding, crowdfunding success increases the visibility of the campaigns inside and outside platforms. More importantly, crowdfunding supports the ventures to develop a customer base from those who contributed to the campaigns. Leveraging this loyal customer base, they enjoy competitive advantages over other competitors starting their operation from the scratch.

Last, crowdfunding success provides important strategic benefits. Most of all, in addition to money from crowdfunding itself, campaigns promote additional funds from outside sources in the aftermath, including VCs, angel investors, and banks. This is because crowdfunding success assures potential market demand for the products from the campaigns. Until the end of 2015, for example, Indiegogo campaigns have raised more than $500 million from investors after the campaigns.[7] In the equity-based crowdfunding context, a study found that 30% of the ventures with successful crowdfunding campaigns pursued one or more equity offerings after the campaigns.[8]

Some pioneering research on "after crowdfunding"

As discussed, the extant literature on crowdfunding has myopically focused on the success of campaigns inside crowdfunding platforms. Most studies focus on identifying important factors that determine project success or illuminate participation behaviors of individual contributors.

Recently, the perspective is expanding to post-campaign phenomena by examining the effects of crowdfunding success on follow-up performance of ventures (Roma et al., 2017; Mollick and Kuppuswamy, 2014). Mollick and Kuppuswamy

(2014) suggest that crowdfunding generates additional benefits ranging from customer input and access to a group of loyal customers to follow-up financing opportunities. Successful campaigns in crowdfunding have been shown to be positively related with ex-post performance (Kim and Viswanathan, 2018). They examined the performance of crowdfunded mobile apps and found that successful crowdfunding in the platform is positively associated with app sales after the campaign, providing some implication of estimation for market demand in crowdfunding. In the equity-based crowdfunding context, Walthoff-Borm et al. (2018) found that crowdfunded ventures have greater innovative performance relative to matched non-crowdfunded ventures while having lower survival rates. Crowdfunded ventures have 3.4 times more patent applications than matched non-crowdfunded ventures.

Crowdfunding may also lead a venture to receive follow-up investments from VCs. Successful crowdfunding can help ventures obtain external follow-up financing because it dampens demand uncertainty about new products and confirms a venture's ability to manage ventures. In this regard, the success of a crowdfunding campaign is likely to be a proxy for its commercial potential and thus serve as a strong quality signal to VCs. Specifically, Roma et al. (2017) demonstrated that obtaining higher amounts of funding in crowdfunding can promote other institutional investors' interest and thus help obtain follow-up financing. But, this positive evidence is effective only when the ventures possess patents or are positioned in a large network of social ties.

In a similar context, Drover et al. (2017) examined how the reputation of the crowdfunding platform and the number of collective contributors influences VCs' screening decisions on crowdfunded ventures. Results showed that the reputation of the platform and the number of contributors are positively associated to the likelihood of being accepted in the screening process. There is also evidence that the link between crowdfunding success and follow-up VC investment is stronger, particularly in the business-to-consumer context (Moedl, 2018). Kuppuswammy and Roth (2016), leveraging survey data on a sample of Kickstarter campaigns, found that money raised by the crowdfunding campaign does have a positive effect on the likelihood of external financing. Crowdfunding serves as a useful tool for probing concepts of the products for creators who seek additional financing. Interestingly, however, this relationship is concave. An in-depth analysis showed the marginal effect of raising additional funds begins to decrease after hitting $75,000.

Our working paper on the topic examines how successful crowdfunding campaigns (compared with the receipt of angel investing) is associated with ventures' subsequent financing outcomes (Ryu et al., 2018). We collected data on crowdfunded ventures as well as angel investing ventures and their subsequent financing from VCs. Our results show that crowdfunding and angel investment, after controlling the difference of ventures, have no different effect on obtaining follow-up VC investments. But, we found that the types of ventures that have been neglected by VCs, such as hardware-oriented ventures and less experienced or less educated founders, could not overcome the disadvantage in spite of their success in crowdfunding. They are less likely to receive subsequent funding from VCs compared to their counterparts. This suggests that VCs are still likely to pay more attention to those crowdfunded ventures that possess traditionally preferred characteristics. Comparing preferences between a corporate venture capitalist (CVC), an equity investment by an established corporation in a venture, with an independent venture capitalist (IVC), crowdfunding success is positively associated with the receipt of subsequent investments from CVCs, whereas IVCs tend to prefer angel financing ventures. This indicates that compared with IVCs, CVCs may be paying more attention to the strategic benefits from crowdfunding, such as knowledge and market demand estimation.

The art of growing a business after (or with) crowdfunding

In 2013, Canary, a hardware venture developing wireless home security systems, set up an Indiegogo campaign.[9] It remarkably raised nearly $2 million, reaching almost 2,000% of its funding goal, $100,000. A difference here from other crowdfunding success stories is that Canary already secured a solid amount of money before launching the campaign. It had raised $1.2 million in seed investment from two hardware investors.[10] In Canary's case, its investors suggested the crowdfunding campaign to promote their investment in Canary and become much more profitable. In fact, it raised the seed investment to make sure that its crowdfunding campaign progressed in a good manner. The seed funding helped them recruit seasoned developers and refine its product design in time for promoting the campaign. It is not surprising that another investor led a $10 million Series A investment round after its crowdfunding campaign.

Recently, several institutional investors have more visibly pushed ventures, especially those developing hardware products, to pursue opportunities in crowdfunding. One of the biggest reasons is that the companies can examine product–market fit and figure out if there is a market big enough for them. Another benefit of crowdfunding is to offer some market estimation opportunities, such as how much cost is required to manufacture and deliver a certain amount of products. Without crowdfunding, those companies might have struggled on deciding initial target prices and production volumes. For those reasons, we could see more collaborative work between institutional investors such as VCs and crowdfunding platforms. For example, Collaborative Fund, a New York-based VC firm is partnering with CircleUp, a San Francisco-based equity crowdfunding platform.[11] They raised the $10 million fund to identify and invest in promising early-stage companies in the retail and consumer product industries. With the partnership, Collaborative Fund could access information on the ventures crowdfunded at CircleUp. The information includes managerial, financial, and marketing data points.

But, it is challenging to turn a successful crowdfunding campaign into a growing venture.[12] For leveraging crowdfunding success to accelerate the growth of a business, key aspects are to 1) fully commit to the fulfillment process of the crowdfunding campaign, 2) continue to grow the community formed throughout the process of the crowdfunding campaign, and 3) upgrade the product according to the feedback from contributors.

For this, most of all, creators are expected to fully commit to the fulfillment process of the crowdfunding campaign itself.[13] As we discussed in the previous chapter, many creators struggle with manufacturing and delivering rewards to contributors in the promised time. Every time, the most effective way to manage unexpected situations that happen during the fulfillment process is to be transparent about them to contributors. The ways of dealing with these kinds of problems after the campaign are important factors influencing expansion and business growth.

Related to fulfillment of the rewards, creators are expected to keep building the community initiated from the crowdfunding campaign. With successful crowdfunding campaigns, creators enjoy the advantage of a number of contributors who are passionate about the product and willing to share it with their friends and family. Creators who want to grow their campaigns into businesses are expected to continue to develop the strengths of the community during and after fulfillment. From the community, additionally, creators can draw attention from potential employees and partners, which fuels growth in the long term.

Last, creators should stay focused on the product onward and upward.[14] One of the great advantages of crowdfunding is the feedback received from contributors. Given the consumer-centric nature of crowdfunding platforms, the feedback gives a valuable opportunity to upgrade products and the business. But, creators are expected to consider trade-offs between benefits from a new feature and adjustment of timelines for launching products, especially for fulfillment of rewards of crowdfunding campaigns. Assessing every opportunity, and how they influence fulfillment capability, is critical. It could be an alternative to satisfy the feedback for a second product version after fulfillment. First, ship the first version of a product. Then, upgrade the product after this successful launch.

As an alternative financing channel, crowdfunding offers new solutions for ventures at earlier stages that have not been sufficiently financed by incumbent investors, and it thus allows those ventures to be relatively flexible in obtaining necessary financing and other benefits at the same time. From the literature and some pioneering cases, we can imagine how crowdfunding can influence the whole structure of the venture financing industry.

Key takeaways

- In addition to fundraising for campaigns, crowdfunding provides additional advantages, ranging from feedback and suggestions from contributors and acquisition of an initial group of loyal customers to follow-up fundraising opportunities. It has the potential to influence the whole structure of the venture financing industry.
- Some institutional investors push ventures to pursue opportunities in crowdfunding because they can examine product–market fit. Crowdfunding also

offers some market estimation opportunities, which is helpful for ventures to scale up their businesses.
- For leveraging crowdfunding success to accelerate growth of a business, first creators are expected to fully commit to the fulfillment process of a crowdfunding campaign. They should continue to grow the community formed throughout the process of the crowdfunding campaign and upgrade the product according to feedback from contributors.

Notes

1. www.kickstarter.com/projects/1316011250/kisa
2. http://mentalfloss.com/article/84237/20-successful-kickstarter-products-you-can-buy-amazon
3. www.indiegogo.com/projects/scanadu-scout
4. https://papers.ssrn.com/sol3/papers.cfm?abstract_id=2376997
5. www.cbinsights.com/blog/crowdfunded-venture-capital-hardware/
6. https://papers.ssrn.com/sol3/papers.cfm?abstract_id=2376997
7. www.vox.com/2015/11/18/11620782/life-after-crowdfunding-startups-that-landed-vc-money-after-online
8. https://papers.ssrn.com/sol3/papers.cfm?abstract_id=2765488
9. www.indiegogo.com/projects/canary-the-first-smart-home-security-device-for-everyone
10. www.fastcompany.com/3035852/how-vcs-use-crowdfunding-to-make-sure-their-hardware-startups-pay-out
11. www.entrepreneur.com/article/273673
12. https://samsungnext.com/whats-next/the-art-of-growing-a-startup-after-crowdfunding/
13. https://entrepreneur.indiegogo.com/education/article/how-to-build-a-business-after-crowdfunding/
14. www.forbes.com/sites/theyec/2014/04/10/what-to-do-after-your-crowdfunding-campaign-ends/#723c2f8a2e72

References

Drover, W., Wood, M. S. & Zacharakis, A. 2017. Attributes of Angel and Crowdfunded Investments as Determinants of VC Screening Decisions. *Entrepreneurship Theory and Practice*, 41, 323–347.
Kim, K. & Viswanathan, S. 2018. The 'Experts' in the Crowd: The Role of Experienced Investors in a Crowdfunding Market. *MIS Quarterly*, Forthcoming.
Kuppuswamy, V. & Roth, K. 2016. Research on the Current State of Crowdfunding: The Effect of Crowdfunding Performance and Outside Capital. *US Small Business Administration Office of Advocacy White Paper*.
Moedl, M. 2018. Is Wisdom of the Crowd a Positive Signal? Effects of Crowdfinancing on Subsequent Venture Capital Selection. *Social Science Research Network*. Available at: https://www.ssrn.com/abstract=3222461.
Mollick, E. R. & Kuppuswamy, V. 2014. After the Campaign: Outcomes of Crowdfunding. *Social Science Research Network*. Available at: https://ssrn.com/abstract=2376997.
Roma, P., Petruzzelli, A. M. & Perrone, G. 2017. From the Crowd to the Market: The Role of Reward-Based Crowdfunding Performance in Attracting Professional Investors. *Research Policy*, 49, 1606–1628.

Ryu, S., Kim, K. & Hahn, J. 2018. The Effect of Crowdfunding Success on Subsequent Financing Outcomes of Start-Ups. *Social Science Research Network*. Available at https://ssrn.com/abstract=2938285.

Walthoff-Borm, X., Vanacker, T. R. & Collewaert, V. 2018. Equity Crowdfunding, Shareholder Structures, and Firm Performance. *Corporate Governance: An International Review*, 26, 314–330.

Epilogue
Divergence and convergence

In the previous parts of BOC, we discussed how, and why, crowdfunding is making the world a better place. Crowdfunding promotes creativity and innovation across the domains (Chapter 5). Diverse stories are being written through crowdfunding campaigns (Chapter 6). It addresses a strand of long-standing shortcomings in the capital markets (Chapter 7). Creators can build new communities and connect to people (Chapter 8). Altogether, it has potential to change our world by eliminating the restrictions in different domains (Chapter 9).

What does the future of crowdfunding look like? Here I would like to share my view on a possible future of crowdfunding in two aspects. First, although the leading crowdfunding platforms keep playing their roles in drawing public attention, we may see the divergence between the platforms for business with scale (e.g., real estate crowdfunding) and those for relatively smaller campaigns in specific domains (e.g., cultural entrepreneurship). Second, the convergence of crowdfunding with different entities, such as established corporations, manufacturers and distributors, and emerging technology, will be escalated. Throughout all these movements, we can see crowdfunding in a wider range of contexts with significant influence on more diverse domains.

Divergence of crowdfunding platforms: business versus community driven

As more entities, either individuals or organizations, are exposed to crowdfunding, leading platforms such as Kickstarter and Indiegogo can expand influence, leveraging their established networks. They will enjoy positive network effects for attracting both potential creators and contributors. As the two platforms are iconic, especially in the reward-based setting, many novices may choose them as an entry alternative toward the crowdfunding world. Those established platforms will perform their jobs in attracting public attention with high volume and unexpected blockbuster campaigns.

In addition to these steady sellers with comprehensive coverage, two distinguished groups of platforms have emerged. The first group of platforms targets businesses with scale. They are more financially oriented compared to the original idea of crowdfunding. For example, a number of equity-based crowdfunding platforms, such as CrowdCube and CircleUp, will keep scaling up to provide clear offerings for business fundraising and investing. There is a lot of excitement around equity-based crowdfunding as it provides ordinary people with an opportunity to invest in promising ventures and make significant returns on the investment. Specifically, equity-based crowdfunding is suitable for a business with a loyal base of customers because it provides shares in return for contributions.[1] Compared to reward-based crowdfunding, both individual and total funding amounts are considerably larger, whereas the number of contributors per campaign may be smaller. Relatedly, real estate crowdfunding platforms such as RealtyShares provide contributors with an opportunity to participate in real estate development.[2] As an individual investor, it is almost impossible to launch a real estate development project. But, real estate crowdfunding has opened the door to development projects and the opportunity to enjoy a favorable return with small amounts of investment. As expected, however, those larger, business-oriented crowdfunding campaigns inherently possess higher levels of risk compared to that of reward-based crowdfunding. The community-like characteristics of crowdfunding would be minimal with this approach. This type of crowdfunding is reaching out to different domains that require considerable amounts of capital to initiate, such as mining[3] and hotel and resort businesses.[4]

On the other hand, a different cluster of crowdfunding has been increasingly atomized, with niche platforms serving specific domains and communities of interest. For example, Seed&Spark, designed specifically for filmmakers, combines the subscription-based crowdfunding model with a streaming service. A portion of each member's monthly subscription fee is allocated to new campaigns by independent filmmakers. Once a creator has a successful crowdfunding campaign and completes a movie, he/she can choose to have it distributed by Seed&Spark. Betabrand, another niche crowdfunding platform, operates as a retail service to support fashion designers. Once a design is submitted, it is shared with potential contributors. The crowd then helps determine if the design can be made by pre-ordering it within 30 days. The contributors get discounts, and the designers can bring their designs to life. This type of crowdfunding platform provides both fundraising and community-building opportunities for creators. Contributors are more cohesive and tend to share more common attributes. They are more likely to perceive themselves as "members" of platforms and possess higher loyalty levels. Due to this community-like aspect, the size of an individual campaign may be smaller compared to business-driven campaigns. But, there are more potential opportunities to launch serial crowdfunding campaigns supported by a common group of contributors. The emergence of Patreon, as discussed in Chapter 5, is a part of this change. Although these platforms pursue and create the value of community building, they are challenged by sustainability issues, mostly due to fewer opportunities for upscaling.

Convergence in crowdfunding platforms: adding more value

Crowdfunding, at the same time, is evolving by converging with different players, domains, and technologies.

First, established companies have started to employ crowdfunding for new product development, especially for those that produce hardware products for individual customers.[5] They realized that crowdfunding can also be useful for themselves in many aspects. Through a crowdfunding campaign, most of all, they can validate their innovation or idea before a mass launch as a way of conducting market research. Although their monetary need is minimal, these companies can observe initial market response from a batch of potential consumers and collect helpful feedback too. Based on the campaigns, they can move forward, or stop, and create and refine a product the market wants. For example, a General Electric subsidiary, FirstBuild, has launched four crowdfunding campaigns on Indiegogo. The Opal Nugget Ice Machine, making chewable ice shards, one among the four, raised about $2.8 million from more than 6,000 contributors.[6] It was one of the most-funded campaigns on the platform. Indiegogo actually has its own service for serving those established companies to use crowdfunding for tapping into new customers, making better decisions, and gaining market insight.[7] Other platforms also offer similar features for those larger companies.

Second, crowdfunding is being connected to production and distribution entities to provide more value to creators. As we discussed, Seed&Spark offers a distribution channel for the films supported on the platform. Betabrand also provides production and distribution support for designers. The mainstream players, such as Kickstarter and Indiegogo, have tried to build the ecosystem for those crowdfunded campaigns by collaborating with professional agencies in related domains, from design to manufacturing to packaging and shipping.[8] Some representative players in the industries also closely collaborate with crowdfunding platforms. For example, Amazon launched Launchpad in July 2015, a marketplace for products made by ventures, including crowdfunded ones.[9] (Amazon has also partnerships with VCs, accelerators, and incubators.) Amazon treats these ventures like any other vendor but also gives them additional benefits such as exposure through customized pages and a website dedicated to the members. So far, major crowdfunding platforms, such as Kickstarter, Indiegogo, and CrowdCube, joined as members of Launchpad.[10,11] Many smaller platforms are joining now. It features a group of crowdfunded products across categories, such as books, movies, electronics, homewares, and more. In the same vein, for supporting filmmakers on their platform, Indiegogo partnered with Vimeo, a premium online video platform. With the partnership, creators passionate about films will be quickly exposed to their potential audiences. Vimeo has also participated in funding for promising film campaigns at Indiegogo in return for exclusive distribution on Vimeo On Demand.[12] As the crowdfunding market expands, the role of those related service providers gets more important, and thus opportunities arise in those domains.

Last, crowdfunding can get more credit by converging with emerging technologies. Blockchain technology will be the most supportive partner among those new technologies.[13] Blockchain technology provides a decentralized, secured, and robust way for information to be stored and distributed in immovable blocks, which is beneficial for crowdfunding in many aspects.[14] The ledger in a Blockchain system allows accurate record keeping for all campaign activity on the crowdfunding platforms, including before, during, and after the campaign. Especially during the fulfillment phase, with a smart contract releasing crowdfunded money only once milestones complete as promised, crowdfunding platforms can reduce the level of risk from falling prey to scams. This high level of visibility into a campaign benefits all players involved. Moreover, Blockchain technology allows contributors to experience more seamless payment. Instead of inserting payment information, a Blockchain-supported crowdfunding platform can provide easier payments with a number of cryptocurrencies.[15] This opens an opportunity to any person with a digital wallet and access to the internet to join the crowdfunding world. The Blockchain payment system is inherently more secure, too. The advanced verification system leveraging a Blockchain identity provides a high level of security. Contributors are not expected to provide sensitive financial information during payment. By providing greater transparency and security with Blockchain technology, crowdfunding can become a more legitimate alternative of funding for a diverse spectrum of campaigns.

Not a game changer, but a change maker

At the end of 2015, Kickstarter announced that it would reincorporate itself to a public benefit corporation (PBC), pledging that it would never sell the company or go for an initial public offering (IPO).[16] Under the scheme, PBCs must aim to do something to help the public and include the goal in their corporate charter. They also must consider public benefits when making decisions and report on social impact. The decision was actually radical in the business world as now it is legally more committing to its mission – help bring creative projects to life – than making profit. It could have tried to sell the company or go public, earning millions of dollars for the founding members and other shareholders, but it hasn't.[17] The idea may cause a disadvantage for Kickstarter to recruit top talent. The related common practice, such as selling companies and going public, attracts talents to ventures with the promise of monetary incentives. Rather, however, it found that the company's stance had attracted more like-minded people – those more focused on the mission than money. Kickstarter has also employed another atypical step in letting employees to exercise their stock options for up to 10 years, even if they leave the company. They also planned to begin paying a dividend to their employers, and shareholders, in the next few years.

From those movements of Kickstarter, the representative of the crowdfunding world, I can see the differences that crowdfunding is making over other financing institutions or even other online commercial platforms. Although it is explicitly about raising money, money is not everything. I don't think, as some experts have already acknowledged, it will completely replace traditional financing as a game changer, but I do believe that it has been making changes by enhancing what is in place. Crowdfunding has real potential to eliminate – or mitigate at least – a lot of the friction that makes the current financial systems biased and thus imperfect. Creators from different domains gain multiple benefits from expanding crowdfunding expeditions, leading to many more benefits for people who want to make our world to a better place with creativity and innovation. No matter what the condition, our world can be improved dramatically when we fully understand *beauty of crowdfunding* and exploit its undiscovered potential for blooming creativity and innovation all around us.

Notes

1. www.entrepreneur.com/video/275696
2. www.moneyunder30.com/should-you-invest-in-real-estate-crowdfunding
3. https://medium.com/unearthed-community/breaking-new-ground-by-crowd-funding-mining-exploration-40efb4065006
4. www.hotelcrowdfunding.com
5. www.theverge.com/2019/4/16/18308523/kickstater-indiegogo-crowdfund-gadget-never-shipped
6. www.nytimes.com/2016/01/07/business/global-brands-taking-cue-from-tinkerers-explore-crowdfunding.html
7. http://enterprise.indiegogo.com
8. www.kickstarter.com/help/resources
9. www.businessinsider.com/amazon-launchpad-started-as-a-crowdfunding-idea-2016-6
10. https://techcrunch.com/2016/07/27/amazon-debuts-a-dedicated-shop-for-kickstarter-products/
11. See www.amazon.com/launchpad/kickstarter
12. https://vimeo.com/ondemand/discover/indiegogo
13. www.crowdfundinsider.com/2019/07/149255-crowdfunding-in-transition-how-blockchain-will-change-alternative-finance/
14. https://eurocrowd.org/2019/04/04/exploring-blockchain-for-alternative-finance-scoping-paper/
15. https://medium.com/pledgecamp/how-blockchain-can-make-crowdfunding-more-secure-427bbccc1eba
16. www.fastcompany.com/3068547/why-kickstarter-decided-to-radically-transform-its-business-model
17. www.nytimes.com/2015/09/21/technology/kickstarters-altruistic-vision-profits-as-the-means-not-the-mission.html

Index

Note: *Italic* page references indicate figures and **bold** page references indicate tables.

achievement motivation 52–53
activeness (campaign characteristic) 57–58
advice (for fulfillment of campaigns) 107–108
age and donor behavior 24
Agrawal, A. 69
Aitamurto, T. 96
Allison, T. H. 32
Alpert, M. 23
altruistic motives 24
Amazon 60, 105, 123
American Committee of the Statue of Liberty 14
American Public Media 89
anchoring 23
angelic backers (contributor type) 55–56
Antonenko, P. D. 31
Arrow Electronics 107
availability heuristic 23
avid fans (contributor type) 55–57

balance (aspect of crowdfunding): capital market and, biased 65–68; children's media campaign and 71–72; gender inequality and, addressing 69–71; geographic bias and, addressing 69; GoldieBlox campaign and 72–73; hardware products campaigns and 64–66; industries and, imbalance across 68–69; Oculus Rift campaign and 64–65; overview 5–6, 8; product-market fit and 66; research on 68–71; Roominate campaign and 72; takeaways, key 73

Barnes & Noble 59–60
Bartholdi, Frederic Auguste 14
Batten disease 89
Bayus, B. L. 32
Beatts, Alan 60
Beethoven, Ludwig van 13
Bennett, R. 24
Betabrand (crowdfunding platform) 10, 122
biological market effect 19
blockchain technology 123–124
blogs 85
Boeuf, B. 31
book publishing 59–61
Borderlands Books (campaign) 60
brand community 26
Brown, Zach ("Danger") 9, 49–50, 77–78, 82
business growth after crowdfunding 117–118
Buttice, V. 81
Byrnes, J. E. 95

Calic, G. 93
campaigns: blogs and 85; characteristics of 57–59; in Chinese crowdfunding platform 80; civic 98–100; community building before kick-starting 82–85; contributors and 44, 52; creativity of 43–44; creators and 52; design/information of 32; employees added after successful 115; Facebook pages and 85; fulfillment of 107–108; information/disclosure of 31–32; journalism 9, 89–90, 92–93, 96–98; linguistic styles of 31–32, 94; newsletters and 85; presence to

audiences, regular and consistent 84–85; scientific research 9, 88–89, 91–92, 94–96; success of 31–32; *see also* post-campaign performance of crowdfunding success; *specific campaign*
Campus section (of Kickstarter) 107
Canary (hardware venture) 117
capital markets balancing 65–68
Carmack, John 65
Cash, Roseanne 90
Castillo, Vina 59
Catapult (crowdfunding platform) 68
Cavallo, Francesca 71–72
challenges/disasters in crowdfunding: Coolest Cooler campaign 105–106; creators and 107; fulfillment of campaigns 107–108; limitations of crowdfunding 110–111; overview 9, 105; risk management and 109–110; Zano mini-drone campaign 106–107
change (aspect of crowdfunding): civic crowdfunding and 98–100; improvement of world and 90–93; journalism campaigns 9, 89–90, 92–93, 96–98; overview of 6, 9; research on 93–98; scientific research campaigns and 9, 88–89, 91–92, 94–96; social entrepreneurship campaigns and 93–94; takeaways, key 100–101; types of changes and 88–90
Chen, H. 66
children's book (campaign) 71–72
CircleUp (crowdfunding platform) 10, 19, 117, 122
civic crowdfunding 98–100
Cleveland, Grover 14
cluster analysis 55
cocreation 42–43, 79–80
cognitive social capital 80
Collaborative Fund 117
collective human behavior 21–22
Colombo, M. G. 32, 81
community building (aspect of crowdfunding) 78–79, 82–85
components of crowdfunding 7, 16–19
connection (aspect of crowdfunding): cocreation and 79–80; community building and 78–79, 82–85; contributors and 79; function of 1; overview 5–6, 8–9; potato salad campaign and 77–78; relationships and, importance of 85; research on 79–82; social capital and, role of 80–82; takeaways, key 85–86
Contagion Theory 21
Conte, Jack 45
contributors: campaigns and 44, 52; in Chinese crowdfunding platform 80; cocreation activity of 42–43; community of potential, defining and reaching out to 83–84; connection aspect of crowdfunding and 79; culturally similar creators and 32; decision-making of, influential factors on 31–32; in donation-based crowdfunding 18; in equity-based crowdfunding 19; journalism campaigns and 93, 96; in lending-based crowdfunding 19; list of potential, creating 84; local 32; matches with creators 32, 56–57, 57; motivations of 54–55; prosocial motivation and 58; in reward-based crowdfunding 19; role of 17, *17*; types of 55–56
convergence of crowdfunding platforms 122–124
Coolest Cooler (campaign) 105–106
cooperative behavior 7, 22
corporate venture capitalist (CVC) 117
Costly Signaling Theory 22
creativity: of campaigns 43–44; defining 41; phases of 42
creativity (aspect of crowdfunding): crowds' versus experts' perception of creativity and 44–45; dimension of contributions 3–5; distribution/commercialization of 15; hardware product campaigns 40; overview 5–6, 8; Pebble Technology Corporation campaign 40; performance of crowdfunding and 43–44; phases of creativity and 42; promoting creativity and 40–41; research on 41–45; Sundance Film Festival and Kickstarter campaign 39; supporting creativity and 41–43; sustaining creativity and 45–46; takeaways, key 46–47
creators: benefits of crowdfunding and 124–125; campaigns and 52; challenges in crowdfunding and 107; community building before

Index

kick-starting a campaign and 83; culturally similar contributors and 32; female 3, 67, 70; independence of 4–5; on Kickstarter 4; literature on crowdfunding and 33; matches with contributors 32, 56–57, **57**; motivations of 52–53; on Patreon 46; post-campaign performance of crowdfunding success and 118; prosocial motivation and 58–59; risk management by 110; role of 17, *17*; social capital of 81; success of crowdfunding and 31; supporting community for 4; types of 53–54; validation of 4
crowd behavior 7, 21–22
CrowdCube (crowdfunding platform) 10, 19, 122
crowdfunding: aspects of 5–6, 7–9; beginning of 1; benefits of successful 114–115, 124–125; business growth after 117–118; as change maker 124–125; civic 98–100; as cocreation process 79–80; community building of 78–79, 82–85; components of 7, 16–19; convergence of platforms and 122–124; defining 16; democratization of capital and 1–3, 78; divergence of platforms and 121–122; financing sources and, traditional 1–3, 5, 8, 33; gender bias and, fixing 2–3, 67–68, 111; growth of industry 1; historical models of 7, 13–15; improvement of world and 90–93, 121, 125; innovation and 1, 3–5, 26; internet and 14; journalism 92; limitations of 110–111; literature on 7, 31–34; marketing advantages of 115; operational advantages of 115; origins of 24–26; players in 17; process 17, *17*; product-market fit and, balancing 66; reader groups targeted regarding 6–7; science, misunderstanding about 91–92; social capital in 80–82; social human behavior and 7, 21–26; strategic advantages of 115; success of 31–32; as two-sided platform 18; types of 18–19; underfunded sectors and 2; understanding, importance of 5, 125; venture capitalists versus, traditional 1–2; *see also* research on crowdfunding; *specific aspect, campaign, player, and platform*

Crowdfunding Center report 70–71
crowd participation in business activity 26
cryptocurrencies 124
customer participation in business activity 25–26

Dai, H. 32
daring dreamers (creator type) 53–54, 59
Darwin, Charles 22
Davies, R. 99
Davis, B. C. 32
decision-making model of venture capital investment 25
De Correspondent 89–90, 92
deindividuation symptoms 21
Deindividuation Theory 21
de Laboulaye, Édouard René 14
Dell Women's Entrepreneur Network 68
democratization of capital and crowdfunding 1–3, 78
design/information of campaign and crowdfunding success 32
Dibb, Josh 107
divergence of crowdfunding platforms 121–122
diversity (aspect of crowdfunding): campaign characteristics and 57–59; contributor motivations and 54–55; contributor typology and 55–56; creator-contributor match and 56–57, **57**; creator motivations and 52–53; creator typology and 53–54; Happy Canes campaign and 49; historical crowdfunding models and 14–15; importance of 59–61; on Indiegogo 51; on Kickstarter 50–51; overview 5–6, 8; potato salad campaign and 49–50; research on 51–59; takeaways, key 61; variety of campaigns and 50–51
donation-based crowdfunding 18–19
donor behavior 24
Drover, W. 116

education and donor behavior 24
e-mail newsletters 85
Emergent-Norm Theory 21
employees added after successful campaign 115
entrepreneurs 1–3, 49; in crowdfunding context 16, 116; female 68, 70–71; fund seeker 53; ideal 25; social 53–54, 56–59, 88, 93–94

equity-based crowdfunding 6, 10, 19, 106, 115–116, 121–122
equity investment 117
Experiment (crowdfunding platform) 9, 89, 91

Facebook 65, 85
Favilli, Elena 71–72
feasibility (campaign characteristic) 5–58
female entrepreneurs 68, 70–71
finance theories (classical) 23
financing sources (traditional) 1–3, 5, 8, 24–25, 33, 64
FirstBuild (campaign) 123
Fried, V. H. 25, 557
Frydrych, D. 31
fulfillment of campaign 107–108
Füller, J. 26
fund seekers (creator type) 53
future of crowdfunding: as change maker 124–125; convergence of platforms 122–124; divergence of platforms 121–122; overview 10, 121

Game Theory 22
gender: bias and crowdfunding, fixing 2–3, 67–68, 111; capital market and, bias in 67; donor behavior and 24; inequality, addressing 69–71; investment behavior and 23
General Electric 123
Genetic Kinship Theory 22
geographic bias (addressing) 69
Gerber, E. M. 42, 52
Giles, Jim 89
Girls in Tech US 68
GoFundMe (crowdfunding platform) 19, 82
GoldieBlox (campaign) 72–73
Good Night Stories for Rebel Girls (book series) 71–72
Gray, Gordon 89
Greenberg, J. 69
Grepper, Ryan 105–106
Griffiths, Simon 88
Group Selection Theory 22

Hagiu, A. 18
Hammerstein, P. 22
Handy, F. 24
Happy Canes (campaign) 8, 49
hardware products (campaigns) 40, 64–66
Harris, Mark 106

Harry Potter (book series) 71
Hassna, G. 99–100
Hisrich, R. D. 25, 57
historical models/projects of crowdfunding 7, 13–15
Homer 13
Hsu, D. H. 25
Hui, J. S. 79–80
Hunter, A. 97

Idaho Potato Commission 50, 77
Iliad translation project 13
independent venture capitalist (IVC) 117
Indiegogo (crowdfunding platform): Canary campaign in 117; categories of campaigns in 8; civic crowdfunding in 99; divergence of platforms and 121; diversity of campaigns in 51; FirstBuild campaign in 123; fulfillment of campaigns and, advice for 107; mentorship programs for women and 67–68; mission of 40–41; money raised from campaigns in 115; Opal Nugget Ice Machine campaign in 123; as reward-based crowdfunding 19, 45–46; Scanadu Scout campaign in 114; Vimeo On Demand and 123; women leading campaigns in 3, 67
indie producers (creator type) 53–54, 59
industry imbalance (addressing) 68–69
information/disclosure of campaign and crowdfunding success 31–32
initial public offering (IPO) 124
Inkshares (crowdfunding platform) 60
innovation and crowdfunding 1, 3–5, 26; *see also* creativity (aspect of crowdfunding)
input suppliers 18
Instagram 45
interest motivation 54–55
internal social capital 81
internet and crowdfunding 14
investor behavior 23
Ioby (crowdfunding platform) 99

Jakubowski, Marcin 88
Jankowic, A. D. 25
Jian, L. 96–97
Johnson, Bobbie 89
Josefy, M. 82
journalism campaigns 9, 89–90, 92–93, 96–98

Kickstarter (crowdfunding platform): Campus section of 107; categories of campaigns in 8; children's media campaign in 71–72; civic crowdfunding in 99; Coolest Cooler campaign in 105–106; creators in 4; divergence of platforms and 121; diversity of campaigns in 50–51; employees added after successful campaigns in 115; experts' perception of creativity and 45; fulfillment of campaigns and, advice for 107; GoldieBlox campaign in 72–73; Happy Canes campaign in 8, 49; historical models of crowdfunding and 14; imbalance in industries and, addressing 68; initial public offering of, possible 124; internal social capital and 81; journalism campaigns in 89; metropolitan areas funded by 67; mission of 40; money raised by 1; Oculus Rift campaign in 40, 64–65, 82, 114; Palmer's record campaign in 46; potato salad campaign in 9, 49–50, 77–78, 82; as public benefit corporation 124; PyroPet campaign in 114; Queens Bookshop campaign in 59–60; as reward-based crowdfunding 19, 45–46; risk management by 109; Roominate campaign in 72; stock options for employees and 124; successful campaigns in 69; Sundance Film Festival and 8, 39; theater campaigns in 44, 82; venture capitalists and 67; *Veronica Mars* movie campaign in 82; women leading campaigns in 3, 67, 69–70; Zano mini-drone campaign in 106–107
Kim, K. 32
Kim, Y-G. 31, 93
Kiva (crowdfunding platform) 19
Kuo, P-Y. 42
Kuppuswamy, V. 32, 115–116

Launchpad (marketplace) 123
lead users 25
Lead User Theory 25
Le Bon, Gustav 21
lending-based crowdfunding 19
LendingClub (crowdfunding platform) 19
Lessner, Matthew 39
linguistic styles and crowdfunding success 31–32, 94

literature on crowdfunding: creators and 33; crowdfunding success and, influential factors affecting 31–32; future research and 33; implications from 32–34; overview 7, 31; post-campaign performance of crowdfunding success and 33–34; *see also* research on crowdfunding
London, Adam 49
London City Hall (campaign) 98
LowLine (campaign) 99
Luckey, Palmer 64–65, 82

Malkin, Pearl ("Grandma Pearl") 49
market advantages of crowdfunding 115
market effect (biological) 22
market performance 4, 13, 33–34; creativity related to 43–44; creator typology and 52–54; ex-post 115–116; social capital and 80–82; sustainability orientation and 93–94
Marom, D. 70
Matter (journalism campaign) 89
Mckesson, DeRay 90
Medium (media platform company) 89
Microryza (now Experiment) 89
Migicovsky, Eric 40
Mollick, E. R. 32, 44, 69, 115–116
monetary behavior 7, 23–24
monetary need motivation 52–53
Mosakowski, E. 93
motivations: of contributors 54–55; of creators 52–53; *see also specific type*
Mozart, Wolfgang Amadeus 13

Nagy, R. A. 23
Nanda, R. 44
National Science Foundation 91
newsletters, e-mail 85
Nikodem, Holly 59
Noboa, Natalie 59
Noë, R. 22
non-altruistic motive 24
non-zero-sum games 22
Norm Theory 22
novelty (campaign characteristic) 57–58

Obenberger, R. W. 23
Oculus Quest 65
Oculus Rift (campaign) 40, 64–65, 82, 114
Oculus VR 40
Opal Nugget Ice Machine (campaign) 123

open innovation 26
open source 26
operational advantages of crowdfunding 115
Oregon Department of Justice (DOJ) 106
overconfidence 23

Palmer, Amanda 46
Parhankangas, A. 94
past experiences and investor behavior 23
Patreon (crowdfunding platform) 8, 45–46
Pebble Technology Corporation (campaign) 40
personality and investor behavior 23
philanthropy motivation 54–55
piano concerto performance project (of Mozart) 13
platform operators 17, *17*
players in crowdfunding *see* contributors; creators; platform operators
playfulness motivation 54–55
Pope, Alexander 13
post-campaign performance of crowdfunding success: benefits of crowdfunding success and 114–115; business growth and 117–118; creators and 118; literature on crowdfunding and 33–34; overview 9–10; research on 115–117; takeaways, key 118–119
potato salad (campaign) 9, 49–50, 77–78, 82
PotatoStock 2014 festival 50, 77–78
product-market fit 66
prosocial motivation 52–53, 56, 58–59
Prospect Theory 23
Prosper (crowdfunding platform) 19
public benefit corporation (PBC) 124
Pulitzer, Joseph 14
PwC report 70–71
PyroPet (campaign) 114

Queens Bookshop (campaign) 59–60

Raiffa, H. 23
RealtyShares (crowdfunding platform) 122
reciprocal altruism 22
recognition motivation 54–55
Reedman, Ivan 107
regret aversion 23
relational aspects and venture capital investments 25
relational social capital 80

relationship building motivation: contributors' 54–55; creators' 52–53; importance of 85
Renko, M. 94
research on crowdfunding: balance aspect 68–71; change aspect 93–98; connection aspect 79–82; creativity aspect 41–45; diversity aspect 51–59; literature on crowdfunding and 33; post-campaign performance 115–117
resellers 18
reward-based crowdfunding 19, 45–46, 122
reward hunters (contributor type) 55–57
reward motivation 54–55
reward value (campaign characteristic) 57–58
risk management in crowdfunding 109–110
Role Theory 22
Roma, P. 116
Roominate (campaign) 72
Roth, K. 116
Rowling, J. K. 71
Ryu, S. 31, 33, 52, 54, 57, 93, 116

Sauermann, H. 94
Scanadu Scout (campaign) 114
scientific research campaigns 9, 88–89, 91–92, 94–96
#SciFund (crowdfunding experiment) 95
Seed&Spark (crowdfunding platform) 122
self-control 23
"selfish gene" 22
Shier, M. L. 24
Shin, J. 96–97
Skirnevskiy, V. 81
societal contribution (campaign characteristic) 57–58
social capital in crowdfunding 80–82
social change motive 24
social enterprises 9, 90
social entrepreneurs (creator type) 53–54, 58, 93–94
social human behavior: collective 21–22; monetary behavior 23–24; overview 7, 21
Social Identity Model of Deindividuation Effects 22
Social Identity Theory 21–22
social status motive 24

Sojka, J. 24
Sorenson, O. 69
South by Southwest Festival (SXSW) 39
Spacehive (crowdfunding platform) 100
Spot.us (crowdfunding platform) 89, 92, 96–97
Statue of Liberty (New York) project 14
Sterling, Debbie 72–73
Stevenson, R. M. 68
Stiver, A. 99
strategic advantages of crowdfunding 115
structural social capital 80
success of crowdfunding 31–32
Sundance Film Festival 8, 39

takeaways, key: balance aspect of crowdfunding 73; change aspect 100–101; connection aspect 85–86; creativity aspect of crowdfunding 46–47; diversity aspect of crowdfunding 61; post-campaign performance of crowdfunding success 118–119
tasteful hermits (contributor type) 55–57
theater campaigns 44, 82
The Correspondent 89–90, 92
Timbuku Labs 71; *see also* *Good Night Stories for Rebel Girls* (book series)
Torquing Group 106; *see also* Zano mini-drone

Tribeca Film Festival 39
Trivers, R. L. 22
trustworthiness (campaign characteristic) 57–58
two-sided platform (TSP) 18

Usher, N. 97

venture capitalists (VCs) 1–2, 24–25, 66–67, 117
Vimeo 123
Vimeo On Demand 123
virtual reality (VR) technology 1, 40, 64–65
Viswanathan, S. 32

Walthoff-Borm, X. 116
Wijnberg, Rob 89
"Women Unbound" (report) 70–71
Woods, The (film, campaign) 39
Wright, J. 18
Wynne-Edwards, V. C. 22

Yousafzai, Malala 71
YouTube 45
Yu, S. 69

Zano mini-drone (campaign) 106–107
Zatko, Maria 88–89
Zhang, D. J. 32
Zheng, H. 31, 80
Zider, B. 25

Printed in the United States
by Baker & Taylor Publisher Services